A

Building
Structures
Primer

Building Structures Primer

2ND EDITION

JAMES AMBROSE

Professor of Architecture
University of Southern California

A WILEY-INTERSCIENCE PUBLICATION

JOHN WILEY & SONS
New York • Chichester • Brisbane • Toronto

Library of Congress Cataloging in Publication Data:

Ambrose, James E.
  Building structures primer.

  "A Wiley-Interscience publication."
  Bibliography: p.
  Includes index.
  1. Structural engineering. I. Title.

TA633.A4   1981   624.1   81-4336
ISBN 0-471-08678-9   AACR2

Printed in the United States of America

10 9 8 7 6 5 4 3 2 1

Preface to the Second Edition

The intention of this revised and expanded edition remains the same as that stated in the preface to the first edition: to provide an involvement with the subject of building structures accessible to persons who lack formal training in the usual background courses of applied mechanics, structural analysis, and structural design. Considering the trends in architectural education, this access has become increasingly desirable, and the trends in both the education for and the practice of structural engineering have made it the only feasible access for many people. Although considerable new material has been added—most notably the chapter on architectural functions—an effort has been made to keep the book small in order to encourage its use by those who approach the subject with some appre-hension. Emphasis has been placed on the use of illustrations and the text has been trimmed to a minimum.

The exercise section has been expanded and developed for use by instructors who intend to employ the book as a text. I am indebted to the vast number of students at the University of Wisconsin-Milwaukee and the University of Southern California whose responses over the intervening years have helped to sharpen my focus on the material. I am also once again indebted to my wife, Peggy, still there after all these years and still giving invaluable help.

JAMES AMBROSE

Westlake Village, California
April 1981

Preface to the First Edition

This book results from my desire to reach a particular audience—those persons who are interested in structures but who have not yet had the opportunity or never expect to pursue a thorough sequence of study in engineering analysis and design. Actually this is my third work on this subject. The first was a set of dittoed notes for a series of lectures for beginning architectural design students at the University of Illinois. The second was a small booklet entitled "Structures Primer," published in 1963 and since used by nine schools of architecture in their early design courses. As this current book has developed I have conceived of it as a springboard into more thorough and detailed work in the subject and I have, therefore, adopted a different tone from that traditionally used. Emphasis has been placed not on the development of engineering design skills, but on the understanding of fundamental concepts and the visualization of the nature and function of structures. Using this approach there is no limit to the subject involvement, no matter how complex or difficult the analysis involved. I believe this is the direction that the education of the architectural student in technological studies must take and I am continually striving to find ways to pursue this approach.

For the architecture student this work hopes to be neither "too little too late" nor "too much too soon," but rather a quick immersion in the totality of the subject—to serve as both an orientation and as a stimulation to more extensive and analytical study. I believe that this work will also be useful to others interested in this subject, such as the industrial designer, the structural engineer majoring in building design, and persons undertaking various courses of study in building design, construction, and administration.

Although the subject is immense, it has been my intent to make this work as brief as possible—the more to encourage its reading! Nothing has been assumed with regard to the reader's background preparation except an interest in the subject. Throughout the book doors are opened a tiny crack, and as soon as the reader's toe is inserted they are slammed shut—and on to another door. For the reader who is really interested in the subject, and who feels a desire and a need for more detail on various aspects of the subject, this will develop a sense of frustration and an unappeased hunger for more information. I hope that some of this frustration may be sublimated into motivation and appreciation for the need for more exhaustive study, to be accomplished in the formal sequence of courses for the architecture student. For the possible use of the student in architecture—but more for those not undertaking such a program—a section at the end of the book is devoted to sources of further information in the form of other books.

The manner in which this book may be used as a text is left to the ingenuity of the teacher. Some suggestions for assignments, examinations, and class projects are given at the end of the text as possible aids in this regard. Portions of this book (or even the whole book, because of its brevity) may be inserted into existing courses, or the book may be used in a whole new course in basic fundamentals in all areas of interest for the student.

I am indebted to many people for their encouragement and contributions to this work. Most of all I am indebted to the students at the University of Illinois, the University of Southern California, and Chouinard Art School, whose reception and reactions to this material have helped to shape its content and approach. I am also indebted to Carl Nelson and Don Sporleder, who first invited me to attempt something of this nature in the beginning design courses at the University of Illinois. Finally, I must acknowledge my indebtedness to the one person without whose help and encouragement this book would never have become a fact—my wife Peggy.

JAMES AMBROSE

Los Angeles, California
May 1967

Contents

Building
Structures
Primer

CHAPTER ONE

Introduction

Most structures exist for a simple purpose: to hold things up. This implies three basic considerations. What is the thing that needs to be held up? What is holding it up? What is trying to make it fall down?

For building structures the thing that needs to be held up is the building or some part of it. What is holding it up is the structural system of the building. What is trying to make the building fall down is a combination of natural forces (gravity, wind, earthquakes, etc.) and forces generated in the use of the building (people walking, vehicles moving, machinery vibrating, etc.).

The purpose of this book is to explain and illustrate all of the considerations just mentioned in terms of their relationship to the design of structures for buildings. Specifically, this consists of answering the following questions:

What architectural functions generate the need for structure?

What loads and effects must structures resist?

How do structures function?

How and of what are structures made?

What are the problems in designing structures?

How can one learn about structures?

1.1 CONCERN FOR STRUCTURE

All physical objects have structures. Consequently, the design of structures is part of the general problem of design for all physical objects, including buildings. It is not possible to understand fully why buildings are built the way they are without having some understanding of the problems of their structures. While the detailed design of structural parts and the actual construction of buildings are usually assigned to others, the building designer cannot function in an intelligent manner without some comprehension of the basic concepts of structures.

1.2 SAFETY

The concept of safety is a major concern in building structures. The two prime safety concerns are for resistance to fires and for a low statistical likelihood of collapse under the loads that the structure must sustain. The major elements of structural fire resistance are:

Combustibility of the Structure If the materials of the structure are combustible, they will tend to contribute to the progress of the fire as well as hasten the collapse of the structure.

Loss of Strength at High Temperature This is essentially a matter of a race against time from the moment of exposure to the fire to the collapse of the structure. If this interval is sufficiently long, the building occupants have a chance to escape.

Containment of the Fire Building fires usually start at a single location. A struc-

Figure 1.1 John Hancock Building, Chicago, Illinois. The tapered building form and exterior X-bracing express the optimization of structure in this 100-story building. The building houses a city within a city: apartments, offices, commercial, recreational, and parking facilities. Architects and engineers: Skidmore, Owings and Merrill, Chicago.

ture that prevents a fire from spreading is highly desirable. The ability of walls, floors, and roofs to resist penetration, or burn-through, by the fire is a major concern in the general safety of the building.

A major portion of building code regulations have to do with aspects of fire safety. Structural materials, systems, and details of construction are rated for their performance in fires on the basis of experience and extensive testing. Building designers must become familiar with these regulations since they constitute major constraints on the selection of materials and use of details for the building construction.

Design of fire-safe buildings involves much more than the consideration of the behavior of the structure. Providing clear paths and proper exits, avoiding combustible and toxic materials, providing detection and alarm systems, and providing built-in firefighting devices—sprinklers, hose cabinets, standpipes, and so on—are all important. The design problem can also be visualized as a race between the fire and the exiting occupants. Figure 1.2 illustrates

the aspects of this problem and some of the things that can be worked on in the design to improve the situation.

The structure must also sustain loads. The safety objective in this case is to provide some margin of structural capacity beyond that strictly required for the actual loads. Thus instead of being not strong enough or just strong enough, the structure should be somewhat stronger than it really needs to be. This extra strength is expressed by the safety factor, SF, which is defined as follows:

$$SF = \frac{\text{the actual capacity of the structure}}{\text{the required capacity of the structure}}$$

As shown in Figure 1.3, if a structure is required to carry 40,000 lb and is actually able to carry 70,000 lb before collapsing, the safety factor is expressed as

$$SF = \frac{70,000}{40,000} = 1.75$$

The desire for safety must be tempered by the need for economy. Although it may be comforting to the purchaser of a structure to have a safety factor as high as 10, the cost of all the extra structure may not be so

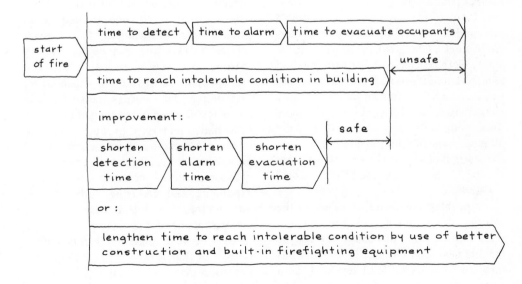

Figure 1.2 Concept of fire safety.

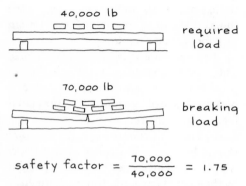

safety factor = $\dfrac{70,000}{40,000}$ = 1.75

Figure 1.3 Concept of structural safety.

attractive. The average safety factor used universally for building structures is 2. There is no particular reason for this other than experience. That is, there have been relatively few structural failures attributed to design mistakes with the consistent use of the average safety factor of 2.

Actually the margin of safety cannot always be established with a high degree of accuracy. As a result, the theoretical 50 percent extra margin of strength implied by the safety factor of 2 is approximate. Nevertheless, it does provide some general protection against errors in the design and construction or in the estimation of the true loading conditions.

In structural design work there are two principal techniques for assuring the margin of safety. One is called the working (or allowable) stress method. With this method the stress conditions under actual usage are visualized and determined by testing or by mathematical modeling. Limits for these stresses are set at some percentage of the ultimate capacity of the materials used. The margin of safety may be inferred from the specific percentage used for the working stress.

A problem encountered in using the working stress method is that most structural materials do not behave in the same manner near their ultimate failure limits as they do at working load levels. Thus a precise prediction of failure cannot be

made on the basis of simple linear proportionality of the stresses. For a true safety factor of 2, therefore, the working stress is often something other than the 50 percent of ultimate stress that might be expected.

This and other difficulties with the working stress method have prompted the use of the other principal design technique, called the strength design method. The basis of this method is simple. The total load capacity of the structure at failure is determined, and the allowable load is set at the desired level simply by dividing the failure load by the safety factor. In the design process, this is achieved by multiplying the actual loads by the desired safety factor and then designing the structure to fail at this design load.

With safety reasonably assured by rational analysis, by testing of prototypes, or simply by experience, a structure may be assumed to be acceptable in terms of life safety. Although this is of vital concern, there are many more considerations that the designer must make in developing a satisfactory structure.

1.3 FEASIBILITY

Structures must be built of real materials using current production techniques. In general this means using products that are on the market and can be handled by existing production organizations and craftspeople. To ensure the feasibility of their designs, building designers must have a reasonable grasp of the current inventory of available materials, products, and processes for building construction. Rapid growth of technology and competition between producers creates a continuously expanding and changing body of such information. Keeping abreast of it is a major challenge for designers.

Just because something *can* be built is no reason that it *should* be. Feasibility is not just a matter of technological potentialities but relates to the overall practicality

client   architect

Figure 1.4 Feasibility and economy: aspiration versus reality.

of a structure. This includes considerations such as the complexity of the design, dollar cost, time required for construction, acceptability of products by code-enforcing agencies, and so on. In some instances the feasibility of even a simple idea may be difficult to establish with reliability.

1.4 ECONOMY

Buildings usually represent major financial investments, and building investors are seldom carefree with their money, least of all for building structures. Except for situations in which the structure is exposed and constitutes a major visible part of the building form and detail, structures are usually appreciated as little as the buried plumbing pipes, electrical wiring, and other hidden service elements of the building. Although investors can be made to appreciate quality in hardware, light fixtures, or finish materials, they are less likely to appreciate expensive foundations, columns, or roof beams. What is usually desired of the structure is simple adequacy in terms of acceptable performance at lowest cost, regardless of the quality or prestige of the building. Hard-working, low-cost structures are generally very popular.

When dealing with economy, it is neces-

sary to bear in mind that the structure, however important to life safety, is only part of the whole building. The aggregate cost of finish materials, doors and windows, roofing, insulation, plumbing, lighting, air conditioning, and so on, may well be several times the cost of the structure. The result of this in many cases is that comparison of alternative structures may be less important in terms of the cost of the structures themselves than in terms of their influence on other factors of the building cost. A particular structure may have high performance efficiency and low cost in its own right but produce forms or details that make other aspects of the building construction difficult and expensive with an end result that is not real economy.

1.5 OPTIMIZATION

Building designers often are motivated by a desire for originality, creativity, and individual expression. Aside from this, or in addition to it, they are also usually striving for the best practical design in terms of function and feasibility. Ideally the aim is for the optimal solution: one that represents the closest fit to the requirements and that compromises least with limitations of cost, time, product availability, code restrictions, and so on. In many instances this requires making decisions that represent balances between conflicting or opposing considerations.

Obvious conflicts are those between desires for safety, quality of finishes, grandeur of spaces, and general sumptuousness on the one hand and practical feasibility and economy on the other. All of these attributes may be important, but often changes that improve one factor tend to degrade others. In terms of the structure, some specific attributes are

Low cost.
Speedy construction.

Fire resistance.

Strength and safety under loads.

Least weight.

Resistance to wear or deterioration.

Ease of assemblage.

Few variations in the design will produce improvement in all of these.

Optimization in real design situations is often elusive since the value of a design can be measured in many different ways. Rank ordering of the various attributes is usually necessary, with dollar cost usually ending up high on the list. Thus the "best" solution often must be qualified in terms of the specific priorities used in the design.

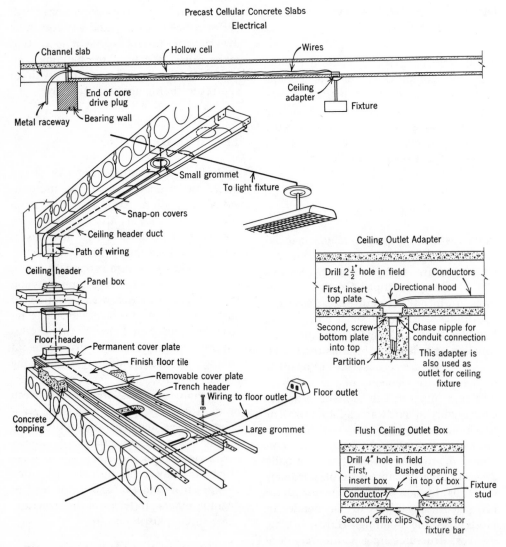

Figure 1.5 Integration of building service systems with the structure. (From *Mechanical and Electrical Equipment for Buildings*, William McGuiness, Benjamin Stein, and John Reynolds, John Wiley & Sons, New York, 1980, with permission.)

1.6 INTEGRATION

Good structural design requires the integration of the structure into the whole physical system of the building. It is necessary to realize the potential influences of structural design decisions on the general architectural design and on the development of the systems for power, lighting, thermal control, ventilation, water supply, waste handling, and so on. Popular structural systems have become so in many cases partly because of their ability to accommodate the other subsystems of the building (see Figure 1.5).

CHAPTER TWO

Architectural Considerations

Buildings serve many purposes and take on a wide variety of forms and details to meet the requirements and fulfill the aspirations of their users. Each building is also unique in its specific combination of location, orientation, and surroundings.

2.1 USAGE REQUIREMENTS

Some primary architectural functions that relate to the structure are

Need for shelter and enclosure.
Need for interior spatial definition, sub-division, and separation.
Need for unobstructed interior space.

In addition to its basic force-resistive purpose, the structure must serve to generate the building forms that relate to these basic architectural functions.

2.1.1 Shelter and Enclosure

Exterior building surfaces usually form a closed, continuous barrier between the interior and exterior environments. This is generally required for reasons of security and privacy and often in order to protect against hostile external conditions (ther-mal, acoustic, air quality, precipitation, and so forth). Figure 2.1 shows the many potential requirements of the external skin of the building. The skin is viewed as a selective filter that must block some things while permitting the passage of others.

In some instances elements that serve a structural purpose also fulfill some of the filter functions of the building skin. When this is the case, properties other than strictly structural ones must be considered in the choice of materials and details of the structural elements. The choice of a particular system of construction often can be determined essentially by factors other than structural behavior. Structural requirements cannot be ignored but frequently can be relatively minor as final decision criteria, and when there are several viable structural options for a given situation, the choice between them often will be made by considering additional factors.

When the need exists for complete enclosure, the structure must either provide it directly or facilitate the addition of other elements to provide it. Solid walls and shell domes are examples of structures that provide naturally closed surfaces (see Figure 2.2). It may be necessary to enhance the basic structure with insulation, water-proofing, and so on, to develop all of the required skin functions, but the enclosure

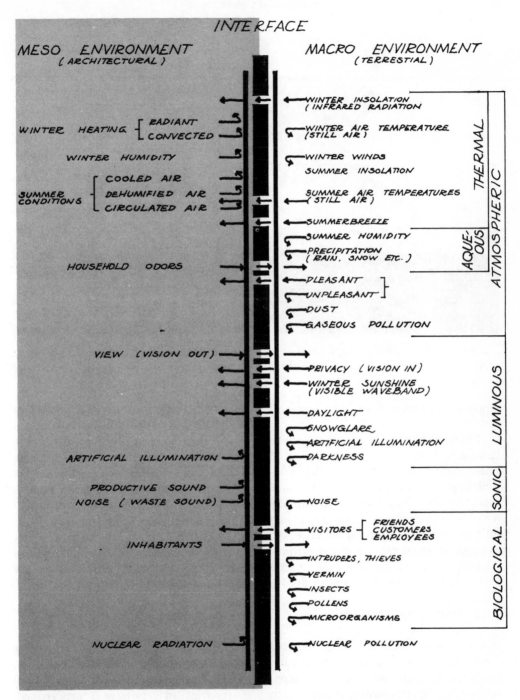

Figure 2.1 Functions of the exterior wall as a selective filter. From *American Building 2: The Environmental Forces That Shape It*, 2nd Edition, Revised, by James Fitch. Copyright 1947, 1948 © 1972 by James Marston Fitch, Jr. Reprinted by permission of the publisher, Houghton Mifflin Company.

Figure 2.2 The self-skinning structure: a concrete shell surface. The St. Louis Planetarium. Architects: Hellmuth, Obata, and Kassabaum, St. Louis.

function is inherent in the structural system.

Frame systems, however, generate open structures that must be provided with added skin elements to develop the enclosure function (see Figure 2.3). In some cases the skin may interact structurally with the frame; in other cases it may add little to the basic structural behavior. An example of the latter is a heavy steel frame for a high-rise building with a thin curtain wall of light metal and glass elements.

2.1.2 Interior Space Division

Few buildings consist of a single enclosed space. Most have interior space division producing separate rooms and often separate levels. The structural elements used to develop these interior forms must relate to the functional requirements of the individual spaces and to the various needs for the separation of spaces. In multiple level buildings the structural elements that form the floor for one level must simultaneously

form the ceiling for the spaces below that level. These two functions generate separate form restrictions, surface treatments, attachments or incorporation of elements such as light fixtures, air circulation ducts and registers, and electrical power outlets. In addition, the floor–ceiling structure must provide a barrier for sound transmission and fire. As in the case of the building's exterior skin, the choice of the construction system must be made with all necessary functions in mind.

2.1.3 Generating Unobstructed Space

Housing of activities creates the need for producing unobstructed interior spaces. These spaces can be very small (small bathrooms) or very large (sports arenas). Generating such spaces involves the basic structural task of spanning, illustrated in Figure 2.4.

The magnitude of the spanning problem is determined by the load and the distance to be spanned. As the span in-

Figure 2.3 Building surface developed as an applied skin: plywood and stucco on a wood frame.

creases, the magnitude of the required structural effort increases rapidly, and the options for the choice of the structural spanning system narrow. The potentialities and limitations of various spanning systems are discussed in Chapter 5.

A particularly difficult problem is that of developing a large unobstructed space in the lower portion of a multiple level building. As shown in Figure 2.5, this generates a major load on the spanning structure. This is unusual, however, and most large spanning structures consist only of roofs for which the loads are relatively light.

2.2 ARCHITECTURAL ELEMENTS

Most buildings consist of combinations of three basic elements: walls, roofs, and floors. These elements are assembled to create both space division and unobstructed space. Before proceeding to consider the structural tasks that are involved in producing these elements we will consider some of the typical architectural elements and the general needs that they imply.

2.2.1 Walls

Walls are usually vertical and therefore lend themselves to the structural function of supporting roofs and floors. Even when they do not serve as supports, they often incorporate the columns or piers that do serve this function. Thus the development of roof and floor structures usually begins with consideration of the wall systems over which they span.

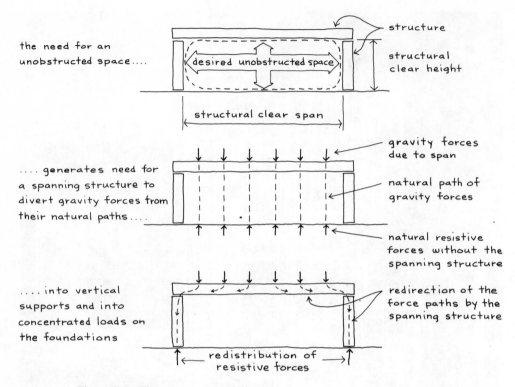

the need for an
unobstructed space....

structure

structural
clear height

desired unobstructed space

structural clear span

.... generates need for
a spanning structure to
divert gravity forces from
their natural paths....

gravity forces
due to span

natural path of
gravity forces

natural resistive
forces without the
spanning structure

.... into vertical
supports and into
concentrated loads on
the foundations

redirection of the
force paths by the
spanning structure

redistribution of
resistive forces

Figure 2.4 The structural task of generating unobstructed interior space.

Walls can be classified in a number of ways depending on their architectural and structural functions. This identification is the basis of many of the design decisions regarding the choice of construction materials and details. Some of the basic categories are:

Structural Walls   These walls serve essential functions in the general structural system of the building. A *bearing wall* supports roofs, floors, or other walls. A *shear wall* is used to brace the building against horizontal forces, utilizing the stiffness of the wall in its own plane, as shown in Figure 2.6.

Nonstructural Walls   Actually there is no such thing as a nonstructural wall, since the least that any wall must do is hold itself up. However, the term nonstructural is used to describe walls that do not contribute to the general structural system of the building;

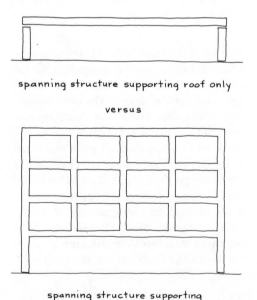

spanning structure supporting roof only

versus

spanning structure supporting
upper levels of the building

Figure 2.5 Load conditions for the spanning structure.

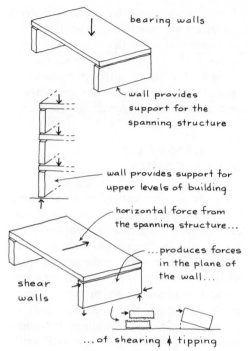

Figure 2.6 Structural functions of walls.

pressures. They may be relatively permanent, as when they enclose stairs, elevators, duct shafts, or toilet rooms, but they are often essentially partitions and can be built as such.

Many walls must incorporate doors or windows or provide hiding places for items such as ducts, wiring, or piping. Walls of hollow construction provide convenient hiding places, whereas those of solid construction can present some problems in this regard. Walls that are not vertical can create problems with hanging objects such as pictures or drapes. Walls that are not straight in plan and wall intersections at other than right angles can create problems in the installation of doors and windows or arrangement of furniture (see Figure 2.7).

2.2.2 Roofs

There are two primary functions that roofs must perform: they must act as skin ele-

that is, they do not support or brace other parts of the building. When they are built on the exterior of the building they are called *curtain walls*. On the interior they are called *partitions*.

Exterior Walls Since they are part of the building skin, exterior walls usually have a number of required functions. Barrier and filter functions are described in general in Section 2.1.1. Wind forces create inward and outward (suction) pressures on the building skin; thus exterior walls must sustain these forces, transmitting them to the lateral bracing system of the building. Exterior walls are usually permanent parts of the building construction as opposed to some interior walls that can be relocated if they are nonstructural.

Interior Walls Although some barrier functions are usually required of any wall, interior walls need not provide separation between the interior and exterior environments and do not sustain direct wind

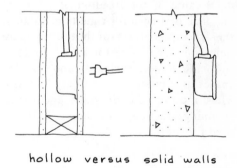

hollow versus solid walls

non-vertical walls

Figure 2.7 Problems of wall form.

ments of the building, and they must facilitate the runoff of water from rain or melting snow. Therefore, the barrier and filter requirements of the skin must be met, and the roof geometry must relate to the gravity water drainage problem. Whereas floors generally must be flat, roofs generally must not be. Some slope is required if water is to drain from the roof surface. The so-called flat roof must actually have some slope; typically a minimum of $\frac{1}{4}$ in./ft, or approximately 1.2° from the horizontal. In addition to the slope provision, the complete drainage operation must be developed so that the runoff water is collected in or dispersed to the gutters, area drains, scuppers, spouts, or other elements that remove it from the roof.

Floors are meant to be walked on; roofs generally are not. Thus in addition to being nonhorizontal roofs may be constructed of materials or systems that are not rigid. The ultimate expression of this possibility is a fabric surface held in position by tension suspension or internal pressure.

Because of the freedom of geometry and lack of a need for rigidity or solidity, the structural options for the roof are more numerous than those for floors. In addition, the largest enclosed, unobstructed spaces usually are spanned only by roofs. Thus most of the dramatic and exotic spanning structures for buildings are those used for roofs.

2.2.3 Floors

Floor structures are often dual in function, serving both as a floor for upper spaces and as a ceiling for lower spaces. The floor function usually dictates the need for a flat, horizontal geometry; thus most floor structures are of the flat-spanning category (discussed in Chapter 5). Required barrier functions for floor structures are derived from the needs of the spaces that they separate.

Most floor structures are relatively short in span, since flat-spanning systems are relatively inefficient and loads are generally higher for floors than for roofs. Achieving large open spaces under floors is considerably more difficult than under roofs, especially since roof geometry is neither flat nor horizontal.

2.3 FORM–SCALE RELATIONSHIPS

There is a great variety of architectural spaces, and therefore there are many different categories of structural problems. The breakdown in Figure 2.8 illustrates variables of form in terms of the interior space division and of scale in terms of the unobstructed span and height or the number of levels. Although this does not cover all possible variations in buildings, it includes many typical ones that are sufficiently different to illustrate a range of structural situations. The following discussion deals with some of the structural problems inherent in the various situations represented in Figure 2.8.

2.3.1 Single Space

This type of building ordinarily represents the greatest degree of freedom in the choice of the structural system. The building basically requires only walls and a roof, although a floor structure may be required if the building is elevated above the ground surface. Some possible uses for such buildings and the potential structural systems are:

Small Scale (10 ft high, 15 ft span)   This includes small sheds, cabins, and single car garages. The range of possible structural systems is considerable, including tents, air inflated bubbles, ice block igloos, and mud huts, as well as more ordinary construction materials and systems (Figure 2.9).

Medium Scale (15 ft high, 30 ft span)   This

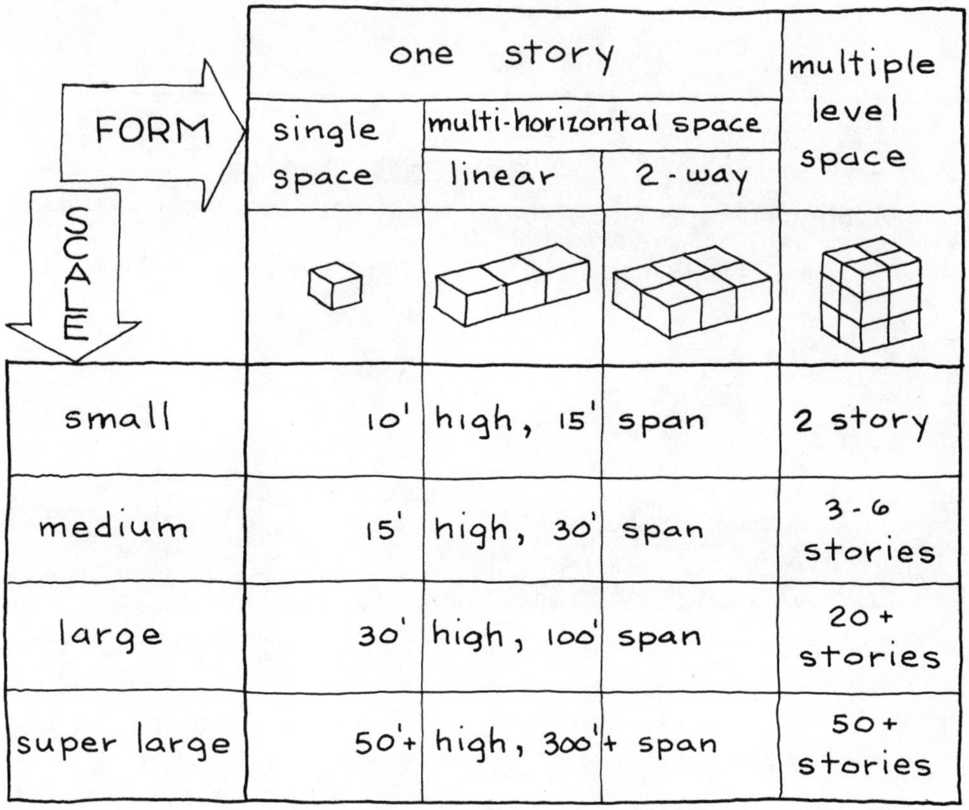

FORM SCALE	one story			multiple level space
	single space	multi-horizontal space		
		linear	2-way	
small		10' high, 15' span		2 story
medium		15' high, 30' span		3-6 stories
large		30' high, 100' span		20+ stories
super large		50'+ high, 300'+ span		50+ stories

Figure 2.8 Problems in form–scale relationships.

includes small stores, classrooms, and agricultural buildings. The 15 ft wall height is just beyond the limit for two-by-four wood studs and the 30 ft span is beyond the usual limit for solid wood joists or rafters on a horizontal span. The use of a truss, a gabled frame, or some other more efficient spanning system becomes feasible at this scale, although some flat decks or beam systems are also possible.

Large Scale (30 ft high, 100 ft+ span) This includes gymnasiums, theaters, and showrooms. The 30 ft wall height represents a significant structural problem, usually requiring a braced construction of some kind. This span is generally beyond the feasible limit for a flat-spanning beam system, and the use of a truss, arch, or some other system is usually required. Because of the size of the spanning elements, they are often quite widely spaced, requiring a secondary spanning system to fill in between the major spanning elements. The loads from the major spanning elements will place highly concentrated forces on the walls, often requiring the use of columns or piers. If the columns or piers are incorporated in the wall plane, they can serve the dual function of bracing the tall walls.

Super Large Scale (50 ft+ high, 300 ft+ span) This includes large convention centers and sports arenas. The wall becomes a major structural element requiring considerable bracing. The spanning structure generally requires considerable height in the form of distance from the top-to-bottom of truss elements, rise-to-span ratio of an arch, sag-to-span ratio of a cable, and so on. (See the discussion of these types of structures in Chapter 5.) The use of super

Figure 2.9 Small-scale, single space buildings serve many functions, including gourmet dining.

efficient structural systems becomes a necessity at this range of span.

2.3.2 Multiple Horizontal Space—Linear

This category includes motels, small shopping centers, and school classroom wings. The linear multiplication may be done with walls that serve the dual functions of supporting the roof and dividing the interior spaces, or it may be done only in terms of multiples of the roof structural system with no interior structure as such. The roof system has somewhat less geometric freedom than that of the single space building, and a modular system of some kind is usually indicated (Figure 2.10).

Although space utilization and construction simplicity generally will be obtained with the linear multiplication of rectangular plan units, there are some other possibilities, as shown in Figure 2.11. If units are spaced by separate connecting links, a higher degree of freedom can be obtained for the roof structure of the individual units.

Structural options of scale remain

essentially the same as those for the single space building. If adjacent spaces are significantly different in height or span, it may be desirable to change the system of construction, using systems appropriate to the scale of the individual spaces.

2.3.3 Multiple Horizontal Space— Two-Way

This category includes factories, stores, warehouses, and large single-story offices. As with linear multiplication, the unit repetition may be done with or without interior walls, utilizing interior columns as supporting elements (Figure 2.12).

Constraints on plan and roof surface geometry are larger here than in linear multiplication. The relative efficiency of rectangular plan units becomes generally higher, although some other possibilities exist. Modular organization and coordination become increasingly logical in the development of structural systems.

Continuity in spanning structures, although also possible with linear multiplication, becomes more useful when the multi-

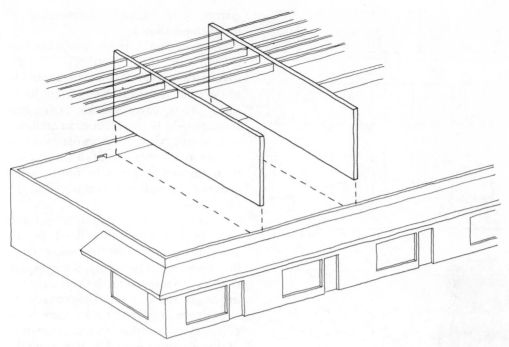

Figure 2.10 Multiple horizontal spaces can be produced with a large number of structural modules, one of the simplest being the repetition of simple bearing walls and roof joists.

plication is two-way. This concept is discussed in Chapter 5 in connection with flat-spanning structures.

Although still possible using linear multiplication, roof structures that are other than flat and horizontal become increasingly less feasible for two-way multiplication. Roof drainage becomes a major problem when the distance from the center to the edge of the building is great. The pitch required for water runoff to an edge is often not feasible, in which case interior roof drains are required.

Structural alternatives related to scale are generally the same as they are for the single space building. The two-way multiplication of very large scale spaces is uncommon, and these structures tend to fall into the medium span category. As with linear multiplication, if adjacent spaces are significantly different in size, a change in the structural system may be justified.

2.3.4 Multilevel Space

The jump from single to multiple levels has some significant structural implications.

Need for a Framed Floor Structure This is a spanning, separating element not inherently required for the single-story building.

Need for Stacking of Support Elements Lower elements must support upper elements as well as the spanning elements immediately above them. This works best if the elements are aligned vertically, and this imposes a need to coordinate the building plans at the various levels.

Increased Concern for Lateral Loads As the building becomes tall, wind and earthquake loads impose greater overturning effects as well as greater horizontal force in general, and the design of lateral bracing becomes a major problem.

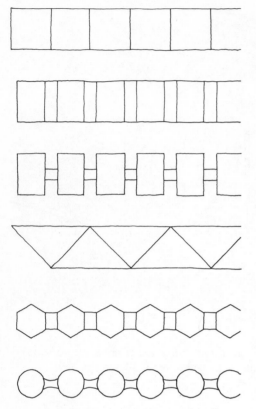

Figure 2.11   Linear plan multiples.

Vertical Penetration of the Structure   Elevators, stairs, duct shafts and chimneys must be carried upward through the horizontal structure at each level, and the spanning systems must accommodate these penetrations.

Increased Foundation Loads   As the building increases in height without an increase in plan size, the total vertical gravity load for each unit of plan area increases. This generally creates a need for very heavy foundations.

The existence of many levels also creates a design problem in establishing a limit for the structural depth of the flat-spanning systems at each level. As shown in Figure 2.13, the critical depth of the structure (*A* in the illustration) is the distance from the top to the bottom of the spanning

system: deck + beams + fireproofing in the example shown.

In many multistoried buildings a ceiling is hung below the floor structure, and the space between the ceiling and the underside of the floor is used to hide various items such as ducts, wiring, sprinkler piping, and recessed light fixtures. From an architectural point of view, the critical depth of this construction is the total out-to-out distance from the top of the floor finish to the underside surface of the ceiling (*B* in the illustration).

The floor-to-floor height, from finish floor level to finish floor level, is this construction depth plus the distance from floor to ceiling at each story. Since the sum of these dimensions equals the total building height and volume, although only the clear space is of real value, there is an efficiency relationship inherent in the ratio of the two dimensions. This constrains the depth allowed for the floor construction, and pure structural efficiency is often compromised in favor of other economic or detail factors.

A critical limit for structural design is the dimension permitted for the largest elements of the spanning system. This limit (*C* in Figure 2.13) must be established cooperatively by the designers of the various building subsystems.

Sometimes it is possible to avoid placing the largest of the contained elements (usually air ducts) under the largest of the spanning structural elements. Some techniques for accomplishing this are shown in Figure 2.14. Large ducts can be run parallel to the largest beams so that only smaller branch ducts need fit below the larger structural elements. If the type of beam used permits it, the beam depth can be varied, and the larger ducts can be placed under the shallower portions of the beams. This is sometimes done with highway bridges. In some cases it is possible to use the full height of the space for the largest beams and to pierce the beams for the passage of ducts.

Figure 2.12 Two-way multiplication of horizontal spaces, achieved here at a medium scale with a common system: steel posts and beams and light steel trusses covered with a light formed sheet steel deck.

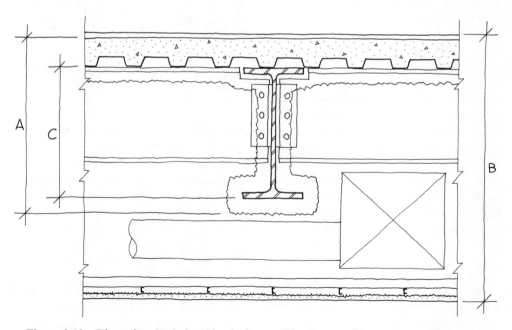

Figure 2.13 Dimensional relationships in floor–ceiling systems for multistory buildings. *A:* total depth of the structure. *B:* total depth of the floor–ceiling construction. *C:* net usable depth for the major spanning elements.

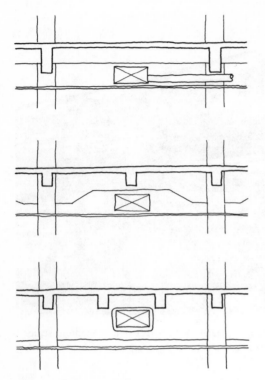

Figure 2.14 Accommodating air ducts in the floor–ceiling system.

An important architectural aspect of the multiple level building is the plan of the vertical supporting elements, since these represent fixed items around which the architectural spaces must be arranged. Because of the stacking required, the vertical structural elements are a constant condition at each level, despite possible changes in architectural functions at the different levels. An apartment building with parking in the lower levels presents the problem of developing a layout for the vertical supports that works for both the multiple parking spaces and the rooms of the apartments.

Vertical structural elements are usually walls or columns, situated in three possible ways, as shown in Figure 2.15:

Isolated and freestanding columns or walls in the interior of the building.

Columns or walls at locations of perma-nent interior features, such as stairs, eleva-tors, toilet rooms, and duct shafts.

Columns or walls at the periphery of the building.

Freestanding interior columns tend to be annoying from an architectural plan-ning point of view, since they restrict the placement of doors and hallways and are usually not desirable objects within rooms. They are also clumsy to incorporate into relatively thin interior walls, as shown in Figure 2.16. They produce lumps in walls that interfere with the placement of furni-ture and the swing of doors. Planning decisions must be made whether to divide the lump between spaces [(c), (e), and (f) in Figure 2.16] or to put the entire lump in one space [(a), (b), and (d) in Figure 2.16].

This annoyance has motivated some designers to plan multiple level buildings with very few, if any, freestanding interior columns. The middle illustration in Figure 2.15 shows a plan in which the permanent interior elements (stairs, duct shafts, etc.) have been arranged to provide the neces-sary interior support for the spanning structure without the use of freestanding columns. The lower illustration in Figure 2.15 shows another approach in which bearing walls have been substituted for interior columns, a solution frequently used for motels, dormitories, and other buildings with fixed, modular room ar-rangements. The latter solution is generally limited to relatively low-rise buildings, since the walls must be thicker in the lower levels if the building is very tall.

When columns are placed at the build-ing periphery, their relationship to the building skin wall has great bearing on the exterior appearance as well as the interior planning. Figure 2.17 shows the five pos-sible positions for columns relative to the exterior wall plane. Each of these options has various merits and problems.

Although freestanding columns (a) are the least desirable, they can be tolerated

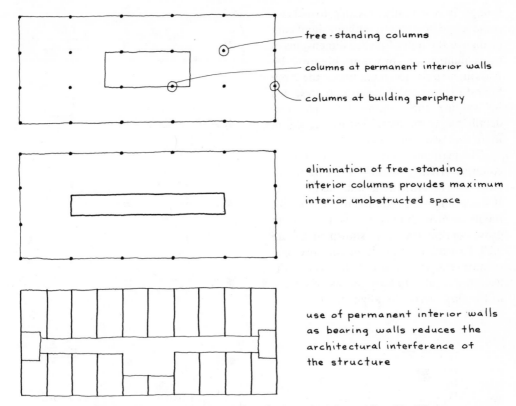

free-standing columns

columns at permanent interior walls

columns at building periphery

elimination of free-standing interior columns provides maximum interior unobstructed space

use of permanent interior walls as bearing walls reduces the architectural interference of the structure

Figure 2.15 Development of vertical supports in multilevel buildings.

architecturally if they are small (as in a low rise building) and are of an unobtrusive shape (round, octagonal, etc.). In some cases they can be treated as features of the design. In framed structures of wood or steel the cantilevered edge usually presents a clumsy problem. In poured concrete structures, however, the cantilever is simply achieved and may even be a structural advantage in that it reduces the stress on the interior spans and aids transfer of force to the columns.

Placing the columns totally outside the wall (e) eliminates both the interior planning lump and the cantilevered edge. A continuous exterior ledge is produced that can be used as a sun shield, for window washing, or as a balcony. However, unless some such use justifies it, the ledge may be a nuisance in creating water runoff and dirt accumulation problems. The totally exte-

rior column also creates a potential problem with thermal expansion, as discussed in Chapter 3.

If the wall and column are joined, three possibilities are shown in Figure 2.17 at (b), (c), and (d), for the usually thick column and usually thin wall. For a smooth exterior building surface the column lump is placed on the inside, although this creates the same planning interference discussed for interior columns. If the wall is aligned with the inside edge of the column, the interior surface will be smooth, but the outside will be dominated by the vertical ridges of the columns. The least useful scheme is to place the column midway in the wall plane, since this produces the same exterior form as (d) in Figure 2.17 while retaining the undesirable interior lump.

In tall buildings, the size of columns usually varies from top to bottom, although it is actually possible to achieve some range of strength without significant change in the outer finished dimensions of the columns, as shown in Figure 2.19. Although some designers prefer the more honest expression of function represented by varying the column size, planning details are often simplified by the use of more uniform column size.

The planning lump problem of interior columns usually makes it desirable to reduce the column size as much as possible. If size changes are required in lower levels, the usual procedure is to have the column grow concentrically, as shown in Figure 2.20. Exceptions are columns at the edges of stairwells or elevator shafts, where it is usually desirable to keep the inside surface of the shaft vertically aligned.

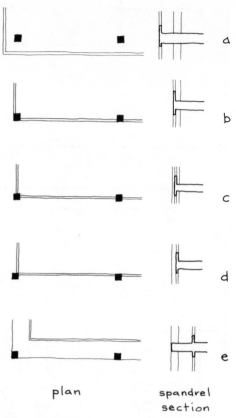

plan   spandrel section

Figure 2.17   Relation of structure to the building skin.

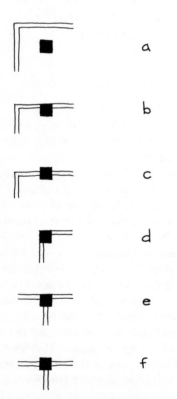

Figure 2.16   Columns incorporated into interior walls.

For exterior columns size change patterns are related to the column-to-skin wall relationship. If the wall is aligned with the inside edge of the column, there are several ways to let it grow in size without changing this alignment (Figure 2.21).

In very tall buildings the problem of lateral bracing for resistance to wind and earthquake forces often becomes a major consideration in the development of the structure and consequently in the development of architectural planning and detailing. In regions of high earthquake probability or frequent wind storms, the lateral bracing problem may be critical even for short buildings.

Figure 2.18 Relative position of the building skin: (*a*) outside the structure, (*b*) in the same plane as the structure, and (*c*) inside the structure, with freestanding exterior columns.

2.4 THE BUILDING–GROUND RELATIONSHIP

As shown in Figure 2.22, there are five basic variations of this relationship.

2.4.1 Subterranean Building

Figure 2.22*a* illustrates a rather uncommon situation that includes such uses as bomb shelters, subway stations, and underground parking. The insulating effect of the ground can be useful for interior thermal control in extreme climates, since the ground temperature stays relatively constant year-round. All exterior surfaces must deal with the soil pressure, water penetration, and deterioration conditions caused by contact with the ground, which strongly limits the choice of materials for the exterior walls.

If the distance below the ground surface is great, the soil load on the roof limits the feasibility of spanning large unobstructed interior spaces. Exterior walls generally will be unpenetrated, although the passage of people, air, and various building services must be dealt with. There is no concern for wind loads, and designing for resistance to earthquake forces is somewhat different below ground.

2.4.2 Ground Level Roof

Figure 2.22*b* illustrates a situation similar to the totally submerged building, except that the single surface exposed to the air offers some possibilities for direct light and ventilation. This condition may be exploited as shown in Figure 2.23 to reduce occupants' feelings of being buried as well as to gain additional light and air.

Roof loading is less critical in this case than in the case of submerged building, although it is likely to have some traffic requiring the use of paving. The weight of the paving plus the load of traffic will constitute a load considerably higher than the usual one for a roof above ground level. The feasibility of large unobstructed spaces will depend essentially on the roof load.

Limitations on materials for the surfaces in contact with the ground are the same as for the submerged building. The roof surface is likely to be penetrated with openings for air, plumbing vents, and so on, and with provision for entry and light, unless the techniques shown in Figure 2.23 are used.

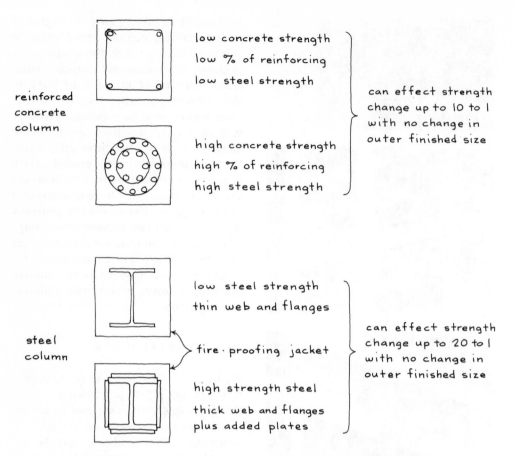

reinforced concrete column

low concrete strength
low % of reinforcing
low steel strength

high concrete strength
high % of reinforcing
high steel strength

can effect strength change up to 10 to 1 with no change in outer finished size

steel column

low steel strength
thin web and flanges

fire-proofing jacket

high strength steel
thick web and flanges plus added plates

can effect strength change up to 20 to 1 with no change in outer finished size

Figure 2.19 Variation in column strength with minor change in size.

2.4.3 Partially Submerged Building

If the building is partly above and partly below ground (Figure 2.22c and Figure 2.24), it often consists of two structural elements: the superstructure (above ground) and the substructure (below ground). The substructure will have all the problems that submerged buildings have. In addition, it must support the superstructure. If the superstructure is very tall, the vertical loads will be high, and a major task for the substructure will be the transfer of these loads to the foundations. The horizontal forces of winds or earthquakes must also be transferred

through the substructure and into the ground.

Substructures are usually built of concrete or masonry. If the superstructure is also built of concrete or masonry, there may be some continuity in the systems of the two elements. If the superstructure is built of wood or steel, the building will literally consist of two structures, one on top of the other.

The superstructure must deal with the various barrier and filter functions illustrated in Figure 2.1. Penetration of the surfaces for door and window openings must be facilitated by the superstructure. The superstructure is externally visible

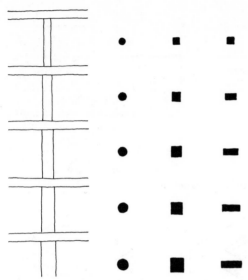

Figure 2.20 Patterns of size increase for interior columns.

while the substructure largely is not; thus the appearance of the superstructure is generally of greater concern in architectural design.

2.4.4 Grade Level Floor

Years ago basements were common. They were usually required for the housing of gravity heating systems and for storage of the wood or coal used as an energy source. They were also useful for prerefrigeration food storage, wind storm shelters, and junk storage. The advent of forced circulation heating systems, refrigeration, and high cost of construction has limited the use of basements unless they are needed for parking or housing of extensive equipment. Figure 22*d* illustrates a building with the floor at grade level and without a basement.

If there is no substructure, the building is reduced to a superstructure and a foundation. If the building is short and vertical loads are low, the foundations can be minimal. If there is no frost problem and surface level soils are adequate, the foundations can extend a very short distance below the ground surface. In addition, if it is functionally acceptable and the ground surface soils permit it, the floor at ground

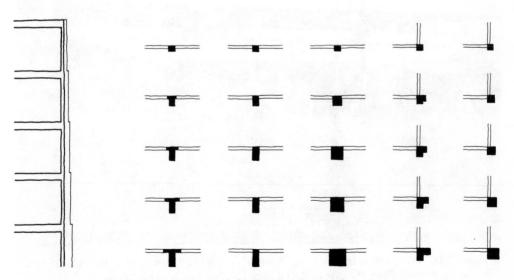

Figure 2.21 Patterns of size increase for exterior columns.

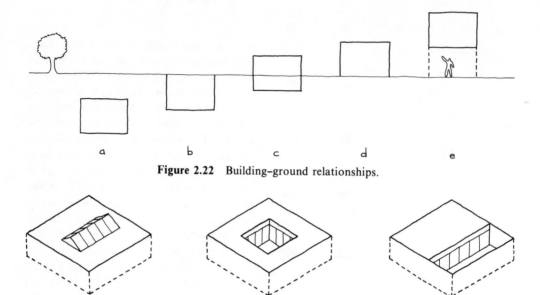

Figure 2.22 Building–ground relationships.

Figure 2.23 Opening up a building with a grade level roof.

Figure 2.24 Partly submerged building. A major portion of the interior space in this building is below the ground. Page Museum at the La Brea Tar Pits, Los Angeles, California. Architects: Thornton, Fagan, Associates, Pasadena, California.

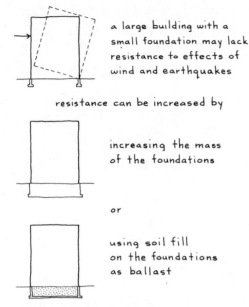

a large building with a
small foundation may lack
resistance to effects of
wind and earthquakes

resistance can be increased by

increasing the mass
of the foundations

or

using soil fill
on the foundations
as ballast

Figure 2.25 Problems of anchoring above-ground buildings.

level can be a simple paving of the ground surface, called a slab on grade.

A problem that can develop with a light building having no basement is that the absence of the heavy substructure critically reduces resistance to the horizontal movement or toppling (called overturn) effects caused by wind and earthquakes. Thus even though only minimal foundations may be required for gravity loads, they would have to be increased in mass or ballasted with soil fill to provide the necessary anchorage for the building (see Figure 2.25).

2.4.5 Above-Ground Building

As shown in Figures 2.22e and 2.26, buildings are sometimes built on legs, are cantilevered, or are suspended from spanning structures so that they are literally in midair. The support structures must be built on or into the ground, but the building has no direct contact with the ground. The support structure may be either an extension of the building structure or a totally independent system.

The bottom floor of such buildings must be designed for the barrier and filter functions of the building skin. In addition, its underside is often visible, becoming an unusual design problem.

Support structures may be quite modest if the buildings they support are not large or imposing. However, if the open span beneath the building is great or the height above the ground considerable, the support structure may become a dominant element of the building. Since most buildings are approached at ground level, the support structure and exposed underside of the building are important architectural design issues.

2.5 ADJACENCY CONDITIONS

Adjacency concerns the conditions that exist at the boundaries of individual architectural spaces. If an individual space is visualized as a box with six surfaces (the top, bottom, and four sides), we can deal with adjacency in terms of the following separate considerations.

Individual Surface Identity Which of the surfaces is being considered: the ceiling, the floor, or one of the walls?

Adjacent Situation What is on the other side of the boundary surface: open air, ground, or another occupied space?

Character of the Surface Is the boundary surface solid, partly open (with a door, window, or open archway), or totally open? If totally open it is not actually a structural boundary but functions as an architectural boundary achieved by visual means, by landscaping, or with furniture or other objects rather than with walls.

Figure 2.27 shows three examples of adjacency situations for a six-sided, box-shaped space. At (a) the space has all six

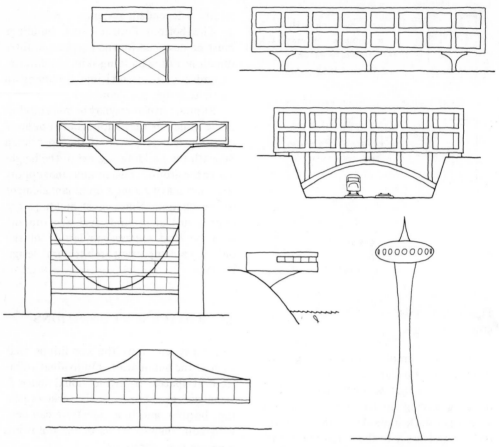

Figure 2.26 Buildings above the ground.

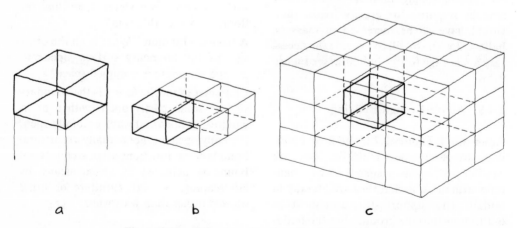

a   b   c

Figure 2.27 Adjacency situations for building spaces.

sides adjacent to open air. This establishes various relationships for the surfaces:

All surfaces are interior–exterior filters.

All surfaces are free of constraints caused by adjacent spaces, except possibly the floor if the space below the building has some functions.

All sides may have openings for air, light, vision, passage of people, and so on.

At (b) in Figure 2.27 the top is adjacent to the air, the bottom to the ground, two adjoining walls to air, and the opposite two adjoining walls to neighboring occupied spaces. This produces a situation in which three surfaces are similar to those in (a), but the others are constrained as follows:

The bottom sits on the ground, eliminating the need for a framed floor, but possibly resulting in problems of moisture, chill in cold weather, frost heave, and so on.

The form of two walls is restricted by the adjacent space use.

At (c) in Figure 2.27 the space is entirely within the building mass with all six sides adjacent to other occupied spaces, resulting in the following:

No possible openings for air, sunlight, or exterior vision.

No need for interior–exterior filter functions.

Some form of constraint on all sides.

Need for dual-functioning top and bottom spanning structural systems, each serving as both floor and ceiling.

The number of theoretical possibilities for the adjacency variations of a single space is enormous. However, practical considerations of use tend to rule out all but a relatively few real situations.

CHAPTER THREE

Structural Functions

In the preceding chapter the role of the structure is discussed in terms of its relationships to the various uses and architectural design considerations for the building. Now let us consider the problems of the structure created in performing its various load resisting functions. The basic issues to be dealt with are:

The load sources and their effects.

What the structure accomplishes in terms of its performance as a supporting, spanning, or bracing element.

What happens to the structure internally as it performs its various tasks.

What is involved in determining the necessary structural elements and systems for specific required tasks.

3.1 LOADS

In the general sense the term *load* refers to any effect that results in a need for some resistive effort on the part of the structure. There are thus many different sources for loads and many ways in which they can be classified.

3.1.1 Load Sources

The principal kinds and sources of loads on building structures are the following.

Gravity

Source Weight of the structure and other parts of the building; weight of occupants and contents; weight of snow, ice, or water on the roof.

Calculation By determination of the volume, density and type of dispersion of items.

Application Vertically downward; constant in magnitude.

Wind

Source Moving air.

Calculation From anticipated wind velocities established by local weather history.

Application As pressure (perpendicular to surfaces) or frictional drag (parallel to surfaces); basically as a horizontal force from any compass point direction, although aerodynamic flow can result in vertical effects on some surfaces.

Earthquakes (Seismic shock)

Source Shaking of the ground as a result of movement along faults.

Calculation By prediction of the probability of occurrence taking into account the history of the area and recorded motions from previous quakes.

Application Back-and-forth, up-and-down movement of the ground on which the building sits; the actual force on the structure is caused by the inertial effect of the weight of the building.

Blast

Source Explosion of bomb, projectile, or volatile materials.

Calculation As pressure, depending on the size of the explosion and proximity of the structure.

Application Highly dynamic inward and outward pressure on surfaces of building.

Hydraulic pressure

Source Principally from ground water levels above the bottom of the basement.

Calculation As direct fluid pressure proportionate to the depth of the fluid.

Application As horizontal pressure on basement walls and upward pressure on basement floors.

Thermal change

Source Temperature variations in the building materials from fluctuations in outdoor temperature and inside–outside temperature differences.

Calculation From weather histories, internal design temperatures, and coefficients of expansion for building materials.

Applications Forces exerted on structure if free expansion is restrained; distortions within structure if connected parts differ in temperature.

Shrinkage Volume reduction occurs in concrete, in the mortar joints of masonry, and in wet clay soils, and may produce forces similar to those caused by thermal change.

Vibration In addition to earthquake effects, vibration or shaking may be caused by heavy machinery, moving vehicles, or high intensity sounds.

Internal actions Forces may be generated by the settling of supports, slippage or loosening of connections, warping of parts, and so on.

Handling Forces may be exerted on elements of the structure during production, erection, transportation, storage, remodelling, and so on. These are not indicated by the use of the structure in the finished building but must be dealt with in the production of the building.

3.1.2 Live and Dead Loads

In building design a distinction is made between so-called *live* and *dead* loads. A dead load is essentially a permanent load, such as the weight of the structure itself and the weight of permanent parts of the building construction. A live load is technically anything that is not permanently applied as force on the structure. However, the specific term "live load" is generally used in building codes to refer to the assumed design loads in the form of dispersed load on roof and floor surfaces as a result of the location and the particular usage of the building.

3.1.3 Static Versus Dynamic Forces

A slightly different distinction is that between static and dynamic force effects. This distinction essentially has to do with the time-dependent character of the force. Thus the weight of the structure produces a static effect, unless the structure is suddenly moved or stopped from moving, at which time a dynamic effect occurs through the inertia or momentum of the mass of the structure. The more sudden the start or stop, the greater the dynamic effect (see Figure 3.1).

Other dynamic forces are produced by ocean waves, earthquakes, blasts, sonic

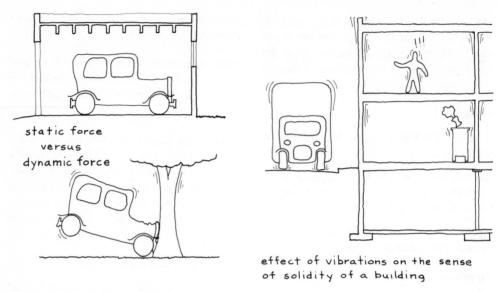

static force
versus
dynamic force

effect of vibrations on the sense
of solidity of a building

Figure 3.1 Static and dynamic force effects.

booms, vibration of heavy machines, and the bouncing effects of walking people or moving vehicles. The effects of dynamic forces are very different from those of static forces. A light steel-framed building, for instance, may be very strong in resisting static forces, but a dynamic force may cause large distortions or vibrations, resulting in cracking of plaster, loosening of structural connections, and so forth. A heavy masonry structure, although possibly not as strong as the steel frame for static load, has considerable stiffness and dead weight and thus may absorb the energy of the dynamic force without any perceptible movement.

In the example just cited, the effect of the force on the function of the structure was described. This may be entirely distinct from the effect on the structure itself. The steel frame is flexible and responds with motions that may be objectionable. However, from a structural point of view it is probably more resistive to dynamic force than the masonry structure. Steel is ductile and the flexible frame dissipates some of the energy of the dynamic load through its motion, similar to a boxer rolling with a punch. Masonry, in contrast, is brittle and

stiff and absorbs the energy almost entirely in the form of shocks to the material. In evaluating dynamic force effects and the response of structures to them, both of these considerations must be made: the behavior of the structure itself and the effects on its usefulness.

3.1.4 Load Dispersion

Forces are distinguished by the manner of their dispersion. Gas under pressure in a container exerts a pressure that is uniform in all directions at all points. The dead load of roofing, the weight of snow on a flat roof, and the weight of water on the flat bottom of a tank are all loads that are uniformly distributed on a surface. The weight of a beam or a cable is a load that is uniformly distributed along a line. The foot of a column or the end of a beam represents loads that are concentrated at a relatively small location (see Figure 3.2).

Randomly dispersed live loads may result in unbalanced conditions or in reversals of internal forces in the structure (see Figure 3.3). The shifting of all the passengers to one side of a ship can cause its

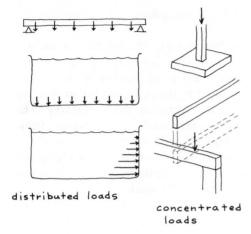

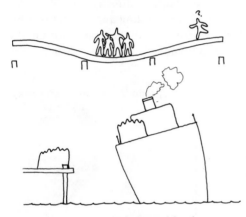

distributed loads

concentrated loads

Figure 3.2 Dispersion of loads.

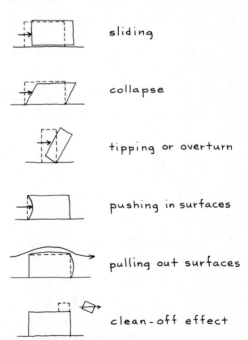

Figure 3.3 Unbalanced loads.

capsizing. A concentration of load in one span of a beam that is continuous through several spans may result in upward deflection in adjacent spans or lifting of the beam from some supports. Since live loads are generally variable in occurrence, location, and sometimes even in direction, several combinations of them must be considered in order to determine the worst effects on the structure.

3.1.5 Wind

Wind is moving air and thus has an impact on any static object in its path, just as water flowing in a stream has a pushing, surging impact on a rock or a pier. In addition to this direct striking force, there are a number of other phenomena caused by the aerodynamic flow of the fluid air. The principal effects of these phenomena are shown in Figure 3.4. The shape and texture of the building surface and the number and location of openings will affect air flow and modify wind effects.

Although for practical purposes gravity is a constant magnitude, single direction force, wind is variable in both direction and magnitude. Wind storms are usually accompanied by gusts, or sudden, brief surges in the wind velocity, which tend to cause structures to rock or jerk. Although usually directed parallel to the ground surface, wind can cause aerodynamic effects in other orientations resulting in inward or outward pressures on any of the building surfaces.

Wind magnitude is measured in terms of the velocity of the moving air. The effect on buildings generally is translated into pressure on exposed surfaces and is measured in units such as pounds per square foot. It is a basic law of physics that this

sliding

collapse

tipping or overturn

pushing in surfaces

pulling out surfaces

clean-off effect

Figure 3.4 Wind effects on buildings.

pressure varies with the square of the velocity, and a formula used for the approximation of wind force on the building is

$$p = 0.003 \, V^2$$

in which p is in units of pounds per square foot, V in miles per hour, and the constant accounts for the units as well as general considerations of the situation. These considerations include factors in the basic physics relationship and the assumptions of an average size building of closed form with flat surfaces sitting on the ground. A plot of this equation is shown in Figure 3.5. Local weather histories are used to establish the maximum anticipated wind velocities for a given location, which are then used to determine the logical design for the buildings in that area to withstand such pressure.

3.1.6 Earthquakes

Earthquakes are the sources of various disastrous effects on buildings. The primary direct effect is the shaking of the ground produced by the shock waves that emanate from the center of the earthquake. The rapidity, magnitude, and duration of this shaking depends on the intensity of the quake and on various geological characteristics of the earth between the building and the center of the quake.

The shaking effect of an earthquake may be a source of serious distress to the building or its occupants. The force effect on the structure is directly related to the weight of the building and is modified by various properties of the structure itself. As its base is moved, the upper structure at

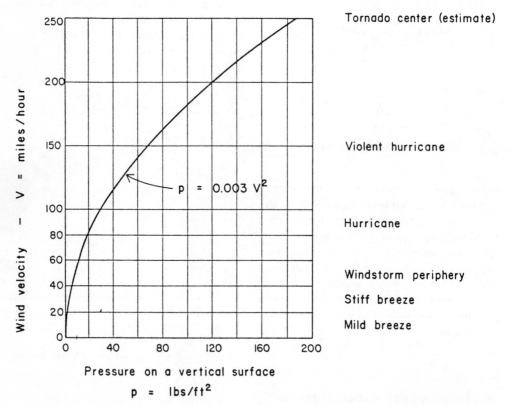

Figure 3.5 Relation of wind velocity to pressure on buildings. (From *Simplified Building Design for Wind and Earthquake Forces*, James Ambrose and Dimitry Vergun, John Wiley & Sons, New York, 1980, with permission.)

first resists moving. This results in the distortion of the structure, since the base is displaced while the upper part of the structure remains stationary. As the shaking continues, the upper portion of the building begins to move and develops momentum. This must be resisted or the building will slide, topple, or collapse.

Continued shaking through many cycles of motion during an earthquake of long duration subjects the building to a complex series of oscillations. If the structure is tall and flexible, modes of vibration may be set up resulting in whiplashlike effects, as shown in Figure 3.6. If the structure is short and stiff, however, its motion will be essentially the same as the ground's. Precise determination of earthquake effects on structures is complex and is only feasible using a computer. Although computers are widely available, the majority of buildings

are still designed using simpler calculations in which earthquake effects are translated into equivalent static forces on the building.

In addition to the direct shaking action, there are other potential destructive effects from earthquakes:

Settling, crackling, or lateral shifting of the ground surface.

Landslides, avalanches, rock falls, or glacier faults.

Tidal waves that can travel long distances and cause major damage to coastal areas.

Bursting of dikes, dams, reservoirs, or large water tanks causing flooding or washouts.

Explosions and fires caused by broken gas or oil pipelines.

It is virtually impossible to design buildings that resist these effects beyond con-

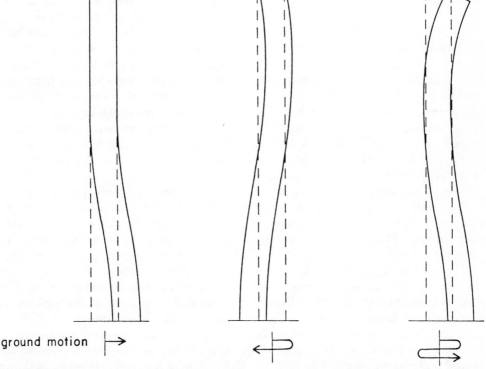

ground motion

Figure 3.6 Earthquake effects on tall structures. (From *Simplified Design for Wind and Earthquake Forces*, James Ambrose and Dimitry Vergun, John Wiley & Sons, New York, 1980, with permission.)

sidering their likelihood in selecting the location of the building. The only security that can be assumed is in low statistical likelihood of the occurrence of such phenomena.

3.1.7 Load Combinations

A difficult judgment for the designer is that of the likelihood of the simultaneous occurrence of various forces. Combinations must be considered carefully to determine those that cause critical situations and that have some reasonable possibility of actual simultaneous occurrence. For example, it is generally considered unreasonable to design for the simultaneous occurrence of the highest anticipated wind velocity and the strongest earthquake. It is also not possible for the wind to blow from two separate directions at the same time, although wind from all directions must be individually considered.

3.2 REACTIONS

Successful functioning of the structure in resisting various loads involves two considerations. The structure must have sufficient internal strength and stiffness to redirect the loads to its supports without developing undue stress on the materials or an undesirable amount of deformation in the form of sag, stretching, twisting, and so on. In addition, the supports for the structure must keep the structure from moving or collapsing. These support forces are called the reactions.

Figure 3.7 shows a column supporting a load that generates a linear compressive effect. The reaction generated by the support must be equal in magnitude and opposite in sense (up versus down) to the combined load, which is the sum of the applied load plus the weight of the column. The balancing of the active loads and the reactions produces the necessary static condition for the structure. This condition

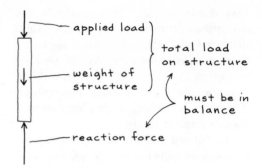

Figure 3.7 Reaction for a column.

is referred to as the state of static equilibrium.

Figure 3.8 shows the reaction forces required for various spanning structures. For the beam the reactions consist of two vertical forces whose sum must be equal to the sum of the applied loads plus the beam weight. If the applied load is not symmetrical, these two reaction forces will not be equal, although their sum must still be equal to the total load on the beam.

For the gable frame the reactions must provide horizontal as well as vertical resistance, even though the load on the structure is entirely vertical. The horizontal forces are required to keep the frame from moving outward at the supports. The net reaction forces are thus combinations of the vertical and horizontal force components required for the complete equilibrium of the structure.

The arch and the cable also require both horizontal and vertical reaction components. When the cable sag or the arch rise is low in comparison to the span, the horizontal component is very large. Thus the magnitude of the force of compression in the arch or tension in the cable may be considerable, even though the vertical load on the span is relatively low.

There is another type of reaction effort that can be visualized by considering the situation of the cantilever beam, as shown in Figure 3.9. Since there is no reaction force at the free end of the beam, the support must develop resistance to rotation

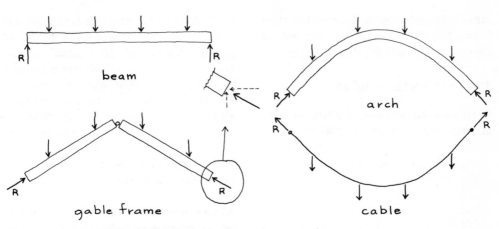

Figure 3.8 Reactions for various spanning structures.

of the beam end as well as to the vertical loads on the beam. This rotational effect is called moment and has a unit that is different from that of direct force. Force is measured in weight units: pounds, tons, and so on. The moment effect is a product of force times distance, producing a unit of pound-feet or some other combination of force and length units. The total reaction of the cantilever therefore consists of two components that cannot be combined: the vertical force (R_v) and the resisting moment (R_m).

For the rigid frame shown in Figure 3.10 there are three possible components of the reactions. If vertical force alone is resisted at the supports, the bottoms of the frame columns will move outward and rotate, as shown in (a). If horizontal resistance is developed, as is shown for the gable, the arch, and the cable in Figure 3.8, the column bottoms can be pushed back to

their original positions but will still rotate, as shown in (b). Finally, if a moment resistance is developed by the supports, the column bottoms can be held completely in their original positions, as shown in (c). For this total resistance to movement at the supports, the reactions must develop all three components as shown.

The applied loads and support reactions for a structure constitute what is called the external force system that operates on the structure. This system of forces is in some ways independent of the structure. That is, the external force system must be in equilibrium if the structure is to be functional, regardless of the materials, strength, stiffness, and so on, of the structure itself. However, the form of details of the structure may affect the nature of the required reactions, as illustrated in Figures 3.8, 3.9, and 3.10. The span and the applied loads may be the same for the beam, the

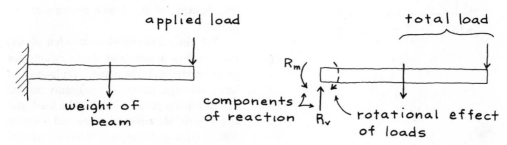

Figure 3.9 Reactions for a cantilever beam.

gable, the arch, the cable, and the rigid
frame, but the required reactions will be
affected by the specific structure.

3.3   INTERNAL FORCES

In response to the external effects of loads
and reactions, certain internal forces are

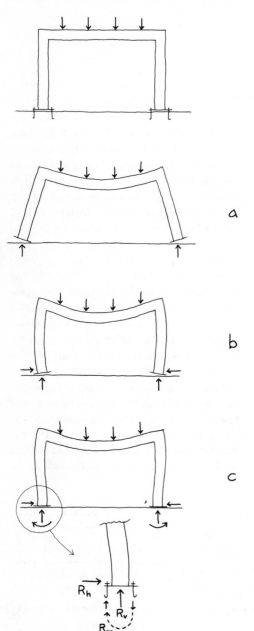

Figure 3.10   Reactions for a rigid frame.

developed within a structure as the material
of the structure strives to resist the deformations caused by the external effects.
These internal force effects are generated
by stresses in the material of the structure.
The stresses are actually incremental forces
within the material, and they result in
incremental deformations, called strains.

3.3.1   Cause and Effect: External
Versus Internal Force

When subjected to external forces a structure twists, sags, stretches, shortens, and so
on. Or, to be more technical, it stresses and
strains thus assuming some new shape as
the incremental strains accumulate into
overall dimensional changes. While stresses
are not visually apparent, their accom-
panying strains often are.

As shown in Figure 3.11, a man stand-
ing on a wooden plank that spans two
supports will cause the plank to sag downward and assume some curved profile. The
sag may be visualized as the manifestation
of a strain phenomenon accompanied by a
stress phenomenon. In this example the
principal cause of the structure's deformation is bending resistance called internal
moment. The stresses associated with this
internal force action are horizontally directed compression in the upper portion of
the plank and horizontally directed tension
in the lower portion. Anyone could have
predicted that the plank would assume a
sagged profile when the man stepped on it;
but we can also predict the deformation as
an accumulation of the strains, resulting in
the shortening of the upper portion and the
lengthening of the lower portion of the
plank.

For the relatively thin wooden plank,
the bending action and strain effects are
quite apparent. If the plank is replaced by a
thick wooden beam, the sag may not be
visually perceptible with a light load and
short span. However, the internal bending
still occurs and the sag, however slight,
does exist. For structural analysis we exag-

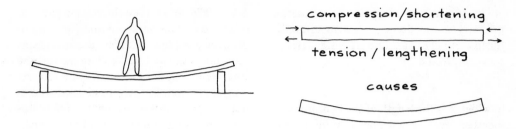

Figure 3.11 Internal bending.

gerate deformed profiles, considering structures to be considerably more flexible than they generally are.

Because the phenomena of stress and strain are inseparable, it is possible to infer one from the other. This allows us to visualize the nature of internal force effects by imagining the exaggerated form of the deformed structure under load. In a further extension of this idea, we may actually quantify the relationship of stress to strain for a particular material and use this relationship in structural load testing to infer quantified stresses from measured strains. Thus although the stresses cannot be seen, the strains can, and so-called stress measurement is actually strain measurement.

Any structure subjected to loads must have certain characteristics in order to function. For purposes of structural action it must be inherently stable, must have adequate strength for an acceptable margin of safety, and must have a reasonable resistance to deformation. These three characteristics—stability, strength, and stiffness—are the principal functional requirements of structures.

3.3.2 Stability

Stability has both simple and complex connotations. In the case of the wooden plank it is essential that there be two supports and that the man stand between the supports. As shown in Figure 3.12, if the plank extends over one support, and the man stands on the extended end, disaster will certainly occur unless a counterweight is placed on the plank or the plank is nailed to the opposite support. In this case the counterweight or nails are necessary for the stability of the structure.

A slightly different problem of stability is illustrated by another simple example. Suppose you have a sore foot and want to use a walking stick to assist your travel. You are offered a $\frac{3}{4}$ in. round wooden stick and a $\frac{1}{4}$ in. round steel rod, each 3 ft long. After handling both, you would probably choose the wooden stick, since the steel rod would buckle under your weight. This buckling action can be readily visualized, demonstrated, and measured. The essential property of a structure that determines its buckling potential is its slenderness.

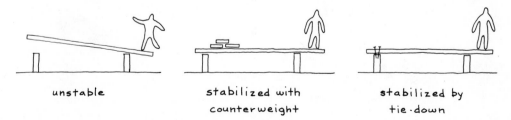

Figure 3.12 Developing stability.

In engineering analysis the geometric property of slenderness used to establish the likelihood of buckling is the slenderness ratio, expressed as

$$L/r$$

in which L is the length of the compression member over which there is no lateral bracing to prevent buckling, and r is the mathematical property of the cross-sectional area of the member, called the radius of gyration and expressed as

$$r = (I/A)^{1/2}$$

In this formula the A value represents the area of the cross section, which is measurable. The I value is an abstract mathematical property called the second moment of the area. This abstract property is a direct indication of the stiffness, or resistance of the member to bending, which is what buckling consists of once it begins to occur. Thus while A merely measures the quantity of material in the cross section, I expresses the disposition of the material in the geometry of the cross section.

In the example of the walking stick, the $\frac{3}{4}$ in. diameter wooden stick has an L/r of 192, while the $\frac{1}{4}$ in. diameter steel rod has an

L/r of 576. If we take the steel in the $\frac{1}{4}$ in. solid rod and flatten it out and curl it up to produce a hollow cylinder, the A remains the same but the I value changes and the stick would now have an L/r of 136. As long as the wall of the pipe-shaped stick is not too thin, this represents a major increase in its resistance to bending or buckling. Figure 3.13 shows the three cross sections of the stick with corresponding L/r values.

Bending and buckling resistance are also affected by the stiffness of the material. Thus a $\frac{1}{4}$ in. rod of wood would be even less useful than the one of steel, since wood is considerably less stiff than steel. For a single, very slender compression member, the compression force required to produce buckling is expressed by the Euler formula, shown in the plot of compression failure load versus length in Figure 3.14. As the member gets shorter, the buckling effect is increasingly less critical, and the limiting effect eventually becomes one of crushing. At this point the limiting compression force becomes the product of the area of material times the maximum stress capacity.

The heavy line in the graph in Figure

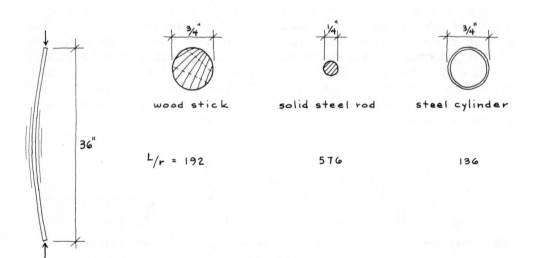

Figure 3.13   Relative L/r values.

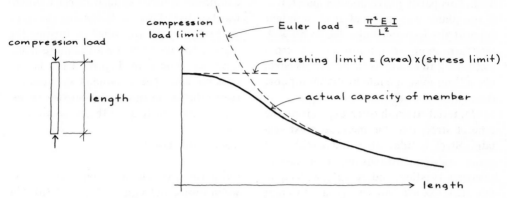

Figure 3.14 Compression load limit versus slenderness.

3.14 represents the maximum compression capacity of the member for the range of lengths from zero to the point at which the buckling becomes so critical that the member is virtually useless for the task. At the short end of this range the curve becomes tangent to the crushing limit as expressed by the area and stress capacity. At the other end the curve becomes tangent to the Euler formula curve. Between these two limits the curve is indeterminate as the member makes the transition from crushing to buckling. In the preceding example the wooden stick and the pipe-shaped steel stick fall into this indeterminate range, while the solid steel rod falls out along the Euler formula curve.

Stability can be a problem with a single element of a structure, such as a single column or beam or a single member of a truss, or it can be a problem for an entire structural system. The eight element framework shown in Figure 3.15 may be stable in resisting vertical gravity loads, but it also must be braced in some manner against horizontal forces, such as those caused by wind or earthquakes. The illustrations in Figure 3.15 show the three principal means for achieving this stability: by using rigid joints between the members, by using x-bracing, or by using rigid panels in the individual planes of the framework (infilling).

3.3.3 Strength

Strength is probably the most obvious requirement for a structure. Even though it is stable, the plank in Figure 3.11 is not strong enough to support the weight of 10

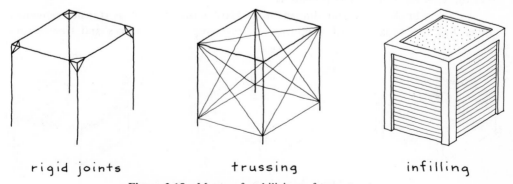

rigid joints   trussing   infilling

Figure 3.15 Means of stabilizing a frame structure.

men. This partly has to do with material—if the plank was made of steel, it might support the 10 men. It also has to do with the form and orientation of the cross section—if the plank is turned on its edge, like a floor joist, it could probably support the load.

Material strength often depends on the type of stress that the material must sustain. Steel is adaptable and capable of major resistance to tension, compression, shearing, twisting, and bending with equal dexterity. Wood, however, has different strengths depending on the direction of the stress in relation to the grain of the wood. As shown in Figure 3.16, the development of major stresses perpendicular to the grain direction can cause the wood to fail easily. Reforming the wood by glue lamination or by pulverizing the wood and producing compressed wood fiber board is a way of overcoming the grain effect.

Stone, concrete, and fired clay are examples of materials that have varying strengths for different stresses. All are relatively strong in resisting compression but are less strong in resisting tension or shear. This requires caution in their use to avoid these stresses or to compensate for them in some way.

Attention must be given to the form and nature of elements and to their uses. A cable woven from thin steel wires has little resistance to compression or bending or anything but the single task for which it is formed—tension. This is despite the fact that the steel has other stress potentials.

A stack of bricks with no bonding in the joints has the capability of supporting compressive force applied directly downward on top of the stack. Picking the stack up by lifting the top brick or turning the stack sideways to create a spanning structure, as shown in Figure 3.17, is not possible since the unbonded surfaces between the bricks cannot develop the necessary stress transfers for these functions.

3.3.4 Stiffness

All structures change shape and move when subjected to forces (Figure 3.18). The relative magnitude of these changes determines a quality of the structure called rigidity or stiffness. The degree of stiffness depends on the materials of the structure as well as on its configuration. Steel is stiffer than wood; wood is stiffer than soft rubber; and so on. Other influences on stiffness include the cross-sectional shape of members, the type of bracing system used, and the nature of constraints provided by supports.

Although stiffness is usually not as critical to the safety of the structure as are stability and strength, it may often be of importance in evaluating the functional usefulness of the structure. If the building rocks back and forth in the wind or if floors sag when walked on, the demonstrated existence of adequate safety in terms of margin of load capacity may be of little consolation to the users of the building.

3.3.5 Equilibrium of Structures

Most structures act as transfer elements, receiving certain forces and transferring

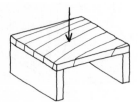  

Figure 3.16 Effect of orientation.

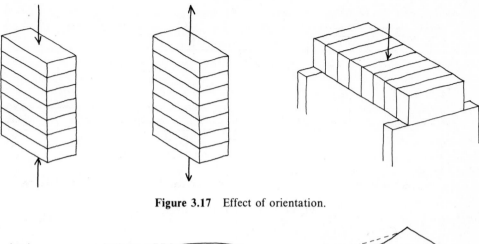

Figure 3.17   Effect of orientation.

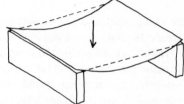

Figure 3.18   Deformation of structures under load.

them to other points. This transfer capability is dependent on the internal strength and stability of the structure. As shown in Figure 3.19, if the structure is a thin sheet of aluminum, force may cause it to crumple or buckle. If it is a block of wood, it may split along the grain. If it is a frame composed of linear members connected by loose bolts, it may collapse. All of these structures fail because of an inability to maintain internal equilibrium through lack of strength or of some inherent stability or both.

The complete static equilibrium of a structure requires two separate balances:

that of the external forces and that of the internal forces. Externally sufficient reaction conditions must be developed at the supports. Internally there must be an inherent capability for stability and sufficient strength to do the work of transferring the applied loads to the supports.

As shown in Figure 3.20, there are three possible conditions for external stability. If support conditions are insufficient in type or number, the structure is externally unstable. If the supports provide an excess of support conditions, the structure is said to be redundant, a condition that is not

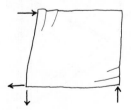

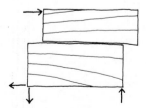

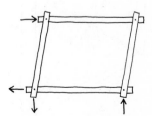

Figure 3.19   Lack of internal resistance.

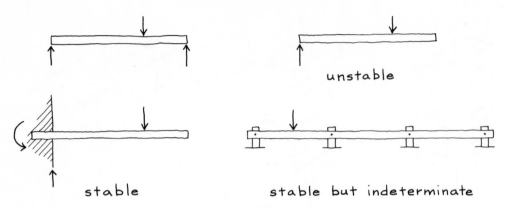

Figure 3.20   Stability analysis.

necessarily undesirable but does somewhat complicate the task of structural analysis.

For internal stability the structure must be formed, arranged, and fastened together to develop the necessary resistance. In the examples shown in Figure 3.19, the aluminum sheet was too thin, the wood block had weak planes, and the frame lacked the necessary arrangement of members or type of joints. All three of these could be altered to make them more functional. As shown in Figure 3.21, the aluminum sheet can be braced with stiffening ribs, the solid wood block can be replaced with a block of alternating laminations with grain directions perpendicular to each other, and the frame can be stabilized by adding a diagonal member.

3.3.6   Types of Internal Force

Complex actions and effects consist of combinations of the following basic types of internal force. The simplest types to visualize are tension and compression, both of which produce simple stress and strain conditions, as shown in Figure 3.22.

Tension   Tension requires particular materials, and certain materials such as stone, concrete, sandy soil, and wood in a direction perpendicular to its grain, do not withstand tension. Stresses can become critical at abrupt changes in the cross section of a member, for instance, at a hole or notch. Tension sometimes straightens or aligns elements. Connections between

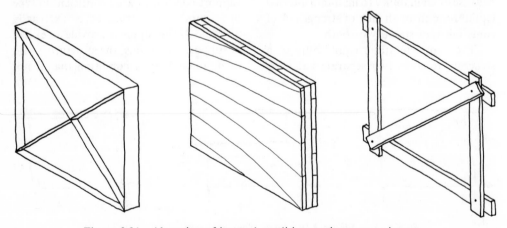

Figure 3.21   Alteration of internal conditions to improve resistance.

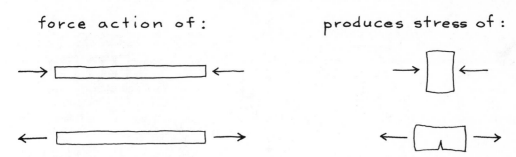

Figure 3.22   Effects of tension and compression.

members in tension are often more difficult to achieve than those that transfer compression, requiring not simply contact but an engagement of some kind (see Figure 3.23).

Compression   Compression usually causes one of two types of failure: crushing or buckling. As discussed previously, buckling has to do with the stiffness and the relative slenderness of the material. Crushing, however, like tension, is related to stress magnitudes and the mass of material in the cross section. Compression can be transmitted between elements by simple direct contact without actual engagement or attachment, as in the case of a wall sitting on a footing or the footing sitting on the ground (see Figure 3.23).

Shear   In its simplest form shear is the tendency for material to slip at the bound-

ary between two points or elements in a structure (see Figure 3.24). If two wooden boards in a floor are connected at their edges by a tongue and groove joint, shear stress is developed at the root of the tongue when one board is stepped on and the other is not. This type of shear is also developed in bolts and hinge pins.

A more complex form of internal shear is developed in a beam. This can be visualized by considering the beam to consist of a stack of loose boards. The horizontal slipping that would occur in such a beam is similar to the internal shear that occurs within a solid beam; thus if the loose boards are glued together, the shear is what must be resisted by the glue joints.

Bending   Tension, compression, and shear are all produced by some direct force effect: pushing, pulling, or slipping. Actions that tend to cause rotation or curvature are in a

Tension:

produces tearing at
holes, notches, etc.

induces straightening
of crooked elements

requires an engaging
type of connection
for transfer

Compression:

produces crushing
of stocky elements

produces buckling
of slender elements

can be transferred by
simple contact bearing
with no engaging connection

Figure 3.23   Considerations of tension and compression actions.

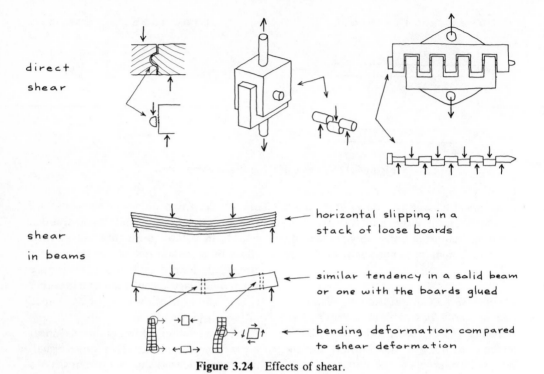

direct
shear

shear

in beams

← horizontal slipping in a
stack of loose boards

← similar tendency in a solid beam
or one with the boards glued

← bending deformation compared
to shear deformation

Figure 3.24   Effects of shear.

separate classification. If the action tends to cause straight elements to curve, it is called bending. If it tends to twist elements, it is called torsion (see Figure 3.25). When a wrench is used to turn a bolt, bending is developed in the handle of the wrench, and torsion is developed in the shaft of the bolt.

Bending can be produced in a number of ways. A common situation occurs when a flat spanning structure is subjected to loads that act perpendicular to it. This is the basic condition of an ordinary beam. As shown in Figure 3.26, the internal force

acting on the beam is a combination of bending and shear.

In buildings, structural movements due to bending (called deflections) are often very high in magnitude, commonly in the range of $\frac{1}{200}$ or $\frac{1}{300}$ of the length of members. In comparison, movements due to tension or compression are usually small, resulting in length changes of $\frac{1}{1000}$ or less in most cases.

Bending may be visualized as being produced by a force acting at some distance from a point. The perpendicular distance from the reference point to the line of action of the force is called the bending arm, or moment arm. The internal force effect that causes bending is called moment and is calculated as the product of the operating force and its moment arm. This produces a unit for moment of pound-feet, gram-centimeters, and so on. Bending is a more complex phenomenon than simple direct force. Since it has spatial connotations involving linear dimensions as well as

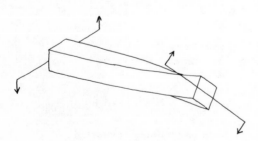

Figure 3.25   Effect of torsion.

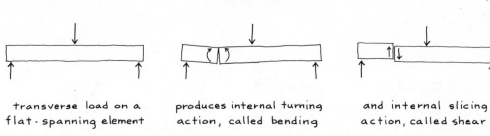

transverse load on a
flat-spanning element

produces internal turning
action, called bending

and internal slicing
action, called shear

Figure 3.26 Internal effects in beams.

force magnitudes, the location of the force is critical in analyzing the effects of bending in a structure. Equally critical is the spatial arrangement of the material or the parts of a structure in relation to the development of internal moment resistance (see Figure 3.27).

Bending can also be visualized as produced by a pair of opposed forces, such as two hands turning a steering wheel. This opposed force mechanism is the way in which a structure develops internal bending resistance. In the spanning plank, for example, tension stresses dispersed in the lower part of the plank oppose compression stresses in the upper part.

Since the development of moment is a product of force times distance, a given magnitude of force can produce more moment if the moment arm is increased. The larger the diameter of a steering wheel, the less force required to turn it—or, with a given limited force, the more moment it can develop. This is why the plank or joist can resist more bending when on edge (joist) than when flat (plank). The farther the separation between the opposed tension

and compression efforts in the bending member, the greater the strength and stiffness of the member. Figure 3.28 shows the effect of form change on a constant amount of material used for the cross section of a beam. The numbers indicate the relative resistance to bending in terms of both strength (as a stress limit) and stiffness (as a strain limit producing deflection).

In addition to the bending created when flat spanning members are transversely loaded, there are other situations in buildings that can produce bending effects. Two of these are shown in Figure 3.29. In the upper figures bending is induced by a loading not in line with the axis of the members. In the lower figure bending is transmitted to the columns through the rigid joint of the frame.

Torsion　Torsion is similar to bending in that it is a product of force and distance. As with bending, the form of the cross section of the member resisting the torsion is a critical factor in establishing its strength and stiffness. A round hollow cylinder (pipe shape) is one of the most efficient

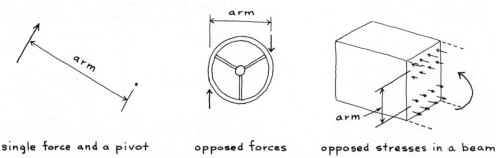

single force and a pivot   opposed forces   opposed stresses in a beam

Figure 3.27 Development of moments.

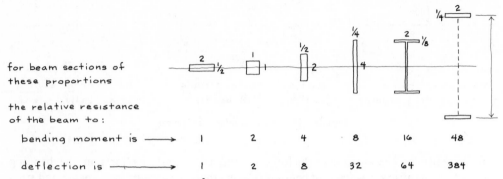

for beam sections of
these proportions

the relative resistance
of the beam to:

  bending moment is ⟶   1   2   4   8   16   48

  deflection is ⟶   1   2   8   32   64   384

Figure 3.28 Relation of cross-sectional geometry to bending resistance.

forms for resistance to torsion. However, if the cylinder wall is slit lengthwise, its resistance is drastically reduced, being approximately the same as that for a flat plate with the same thickness. Figure 3.30 shows the effect on torsional resistance of variations in the cross-sectional shape of a linear member with the same amount of material.

Often in designing structures it is better to develop resistance to torsional effects by bracing members against the twisting actions. Thus the torsional effect is absorbed by the bracing rather than by stresses in the twisted member.

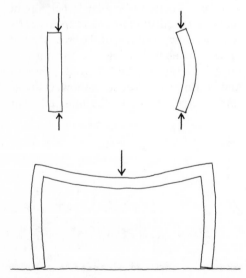

Figure 3.29 Conditions resulting in internal bending.

3.3.7 Combinations of Internal Forces

The individual actions of tension, compression, shear, bending, and torsion can occur in various combinations and in several directions at a single location in a structure. As illustrated previously, beams ordinarily sustain a combination of bending and shear. In the vertical members of the frame shown in Figure 3.29 the loading will produce a combination of internal compression, bending, and shear. In the example shown in Figure 3.31 the loading will produce a combination of compression, bending, torsion, and shear in the vertical member. Structures must be analyzed carefully for the various internal force combinations that occur and for the critical maximum stresses and deformations that result from the combined force actions. In addition, the external loads may occur in different combinations, each producing its own combined internal actions. In these situations the analysis of structural behavior and design of the structural members can become very complex and laborious.

3.4 STRESS AND STRAIN

Internal force actions are resisted by stresses in the material of the structure. There are three basic types of stress: tension, compression, and shear. Tension and compression are similar in nature, although

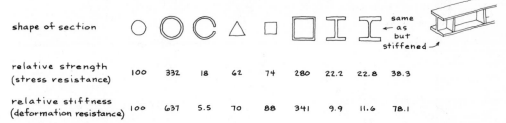

shape of section

relative strength (stress resistance)	100	332	18	62	74	280	22.2	22.8	38.3
relative stiffness (deformation resistance)	100	637	5.5	70	88	341	9.9	11.6	78.1

Figure 3.30 Relation of cross-sectional geometry to torsional resistance. (From "Structural Beams in Torsion," Inge Lyse and Bruce Johnson, *Transactions of the ASCE*, **101**, 1936, American Society of Civil Engineers, with permission.)

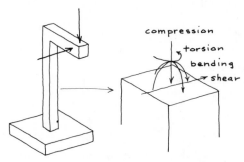

Figure 3.31 Combined internal force effects.

opposite in sign or direction. Both tension and compression produce a linear type of strain and can be visualized as pressure effects perpendicular to the surface of a stressed cross section, as shown in Figure 3.32. Because of these similarities, both tension and compression stress are referred to as direct stresses, one considered positive and the other negative.

Shear stress occurs in the plane of a cross section and is similar to a friction effect. As shown in Figure 3.33, strain due

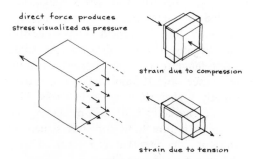

Figure 3.32 Direct stress and strain.

to shear stress is different from that due to direct stress: it consists of an angular change rather than a linear shortening or lengthening.

3.4.1 Stress–Strain Relations

Stress and strain are related not only in the basic forms that they take, but also in their actual magnitudes. Figure 3.34 shows the relation between stress and strain for a number of different materials. The form of such a graph illustrates various aspects of the nature of the material.

Curves 1 and 2 represent so-called *elastic* materials; the straight line form indicating a constant proportionality of the stress and strain magnitudes. For these materials the relation of stress to strain can be quantified simply in terms of the slope, or angle, of the graph. This relationship is commonly expressed in the form of the tangent of the angle of the graph and is called the *modulus of elasticity* of the material. The higher this modulus—that is, the steeper the angle—the stiffer the material. Thus the material represented by curve 1 in the illustration is stiffer than the material represented by curve 2.

For direct stress of tension or compression the strain is measured as a linear change, and the modulus is called the direct stress modulus of elasticity. For shear stress the strain is measured as angular change, and the resulting modulus is called the shear stress modulus of elasticity.

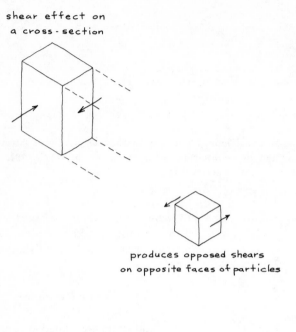

Figure 3.33   Shear stress and strain.

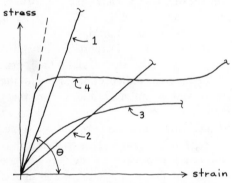

Figure 3.34   Stress–strain relationships.

Some materials, such as glass and very high strength steel, behave almost purely elastically, having a constant modulus of elasticity for the whole range of stress up to failure of the material. Other materials, such as wood, concrete, and most soft plastics, have a curved form in the stress–strain graph (curve 3 in Figure 3.34). This indicates that the modulus varies continu-ously throughout the stress range. For such materials the modulus is expressed as a tangent to the curve at some particular point (a specific stress magnitude) or as an average for the stress range between two specific points.

The odd shape of curve 4 in Figure 3.34 is the characteristic form for the stress–strain graph for a so-called *ductile* mate-rial, such as low grade steel of the type commonly used for beams and columns in buildings. This material behaves essentially elastically up to some stress magnitude (called the yield stress), at which point it suddenly deforms considerably while still maintaining stress resistance. At some strain magnitude it again develops a strain resistance and finally fails at a stress slightly higher than the yield stress. This ductile character is used in predicting the ultimate failure limit for steel structures and for concrete that is reinforced with low-grade reinforcing bars.

3.4.2 Stress Combinations

Stress and strain are actually three-dimensional phenomena, although for simplicity they are often visualized in linear or planar form. As shown in Figure 3.32, direct stress of compression in a single direction results in a strain consisting of shortening of the material in that direction. However, if the volume of the material remains essentially unchanged, which it usually does, there will be a resulting effect of lengthening (or pushing out) at right angles to the compression stress. This implies the development of a tension effect at right angles to the compression, and this effect is sometimes the actual source of material failure when the material is relatively weak in tension, as is the case of concrete. Thus a common form of failure for concrete in compression is by lateral bursting at right angles to the compression.

If direct stress is induced in a linear member, as shown in Figure 3.35, the pure direct stress occurs only on cross sections at right angles to the direct force effect. If stress is considered on a cross section at some other angle, there will be a component of shear on the cross section. If the material is weak in shear, this angular shear stress effect may be more critical than the direct stress effect.

Although simple linear tension and compression forces produce direct, linear stresses, shear stress is essentially two-dimensional, as shown in Figure 3.36. The effect of shear force produces shear stresses (shown in the figure on faces *a* and *b* of a particle of material), resulting in a rota-

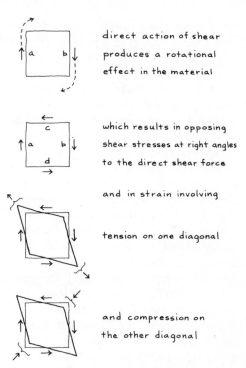

direct action of shear produces a rotational effect in the material

which results in opposing shear stresses at right angles to the direct shear force

and in strain involving

tension on one diagonal

and compression on the other diagonal

Figure 3.36 Effects of shear.

tional effect on the material. This rotational effect must be counteracted by the development of opposing shear stresses (faces *c* and *d*) resulting in the development of a shear stress at right angles to the original shear effect. Thus whenever shear stress exists within a structure, there is always an equal magnitude of shear stress at right angles to it. An example of this is the stack of loose boards used as a beam (Figure 3.24). The shear failure in this case is a horizontal slipping effect between the boards, even though the direct shear is induced by a vertical loading.

As shown in Figure 3.36, the combination of the mutually perpendicular shear stresses results in a lengthening of the material in one diagonal direction and a shortening in the other diagonal direction at right angles to the lengthening. These are called the diagonal stress effects, since they literally result in tension in one diagonal direction and compression in the other direction. In some situations these diago-

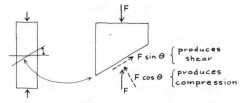

$F \sin \theta$ { produces shear
$F \cos \theta$ { produces compression

Figure 3.35 Stress on a cross section not at right angles to the active force.

nal stresses will be more critical than the direct shear stresses that produce them. In concrete, for example, failure due to shear effects is usually actually a tension failure, since this is the weakest stress property of the material. In the thin webs of steel beams diagonal compression caused by shear can cause a buckling of the web well below the actual shear stress limit of the steel.

Direct stresses of tension and compression in a single direction are summed algebraically at a given point in the structure. In the case of the column shown in Figure 3.37, the compression load produces a direct compression stress on a cross section, as shown at (a), if the load is placed so as not to produce bending. If the load is off-center on the column, the stress condition will be modified by the addition of bending stresses, which will be distributed on the cross section as shown at (b), with a range from compression to tension on the opposite sides of the section. The true net stress condition is shown at (c), consisting of the simple addition of the two stress conditions [(a) and (b)].

A more complex situation is the combination of direct stresses and shear stresses. Figure 3.38 shows the general condition at a point in the cross section of a beam where the net stress consists of a combination of bending stress [as shown for the column in (b) of Figure 3.37] and shear stress. These two types of stress cannot be combined directly. What is combined is the direct stress (bending) and the diagonal stresses (shear), as shown in (b) and (c) in the illustration. Since these stresses are not in the same direction, they must be combined vectorially, producing a vector-resultant stress at some different angle from either of the two basic stresses. There is also a net combined shear stress, as shown at (d) in Figure 3.38. This consists of a vector addition of the shear on a diagonal cross section due to the bending stress plus the shear due to the direct internal shear force. Again, the net stress will occur on a plane at some compromise angle. The

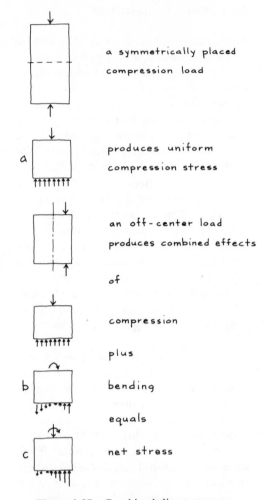

Figure 3.37 Combined direct stresses.

manner in which these net stresses are dispersed throughout the length of a beam is discussed in the section on flat-spanning systems in Chapter 5.

Another stress combination is that produced by biaxial or triaxial stress conditions. An example of this, as shown in Figure 3.39, is the condition that occurs when a material is confined, such as when air or liquid is squeezed in a piston chamber. The confinement results in a resistance at right angles to the direct compression effort. The net effect on the material is a three-way push, or a triaxial compression. For materials with virtually no tensile

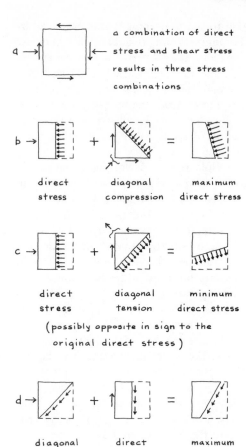

Figure 3.38 Combined shear stress and direct stress.

resistance such as air, water, or dry sand, this is the only type of situation in which they can develop resistance to compression. Thus the sand beneath a footing can develop compressive resistance because of the confinement offered by the surrounding soil. If the footing is on top of the mound of sand, it will sink because the sand is not confined.

3.4.3 Thermal Stresses

The volumes of solid materials change with temperature variation, increasing as the temperature is raised and decreasing as it is lowered. This phenomenon creates a number of problems that must be dealt with in building design.

The form of objects determines the basic nature of the dimensional changes. As shown in Figure 3.40, the critical directions of movement depend on whether the object is essentially linear, planar, or three-dimensional. For a linear object the major significant change is in its length. Thus linear framing members, roof edge trim, and so on, experience considerable length change if they are long and are subjected to a large temperature range through exposure to the climate.

Planar objects, such as wall panels or

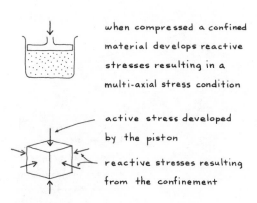

Figure 3.39 Development of stress in a confined material.

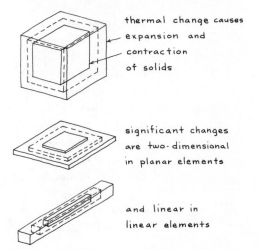

Figure 3.40 Effects of thermal change on solids.

large sheets of glass, expand in a two-dimensional manner. Attachments or edge constraints for such objects must deal with this type of movement. A window frame must hold the glass in a manner that allows some movement of the glass within it. Long or tall wall surfaces must accommodate thermal movements, usually by providing expansion joints at intervals to reduce the length over which movement accumulates.

If thermal expansion or contraction is resisted, stresses are produced in the structure. Figure 3.41 shows a linear structural member in which length change is constrained. If the temperature is raised, the member will push outward against the constraints, developing compression stress as the constraints push back. This is directly analogous to applying an external compressive force. The magnitude of this compression can be calculated by equating the dimension of the free thermal expan-

sion to the shortening that is produced by the compression. If quantified values are known for the properties of thermal expansion and the stress–strain relationship for the material, a quantified stress can be determined from the temperature change. Summation of this unit stress on the cross section of the member produces the compression force.

While there are various situations in which simple expansion and contraction itself is the problem, there are other situations in which the problem is one of differential movements. Figure 3.42 shows a common situation that occurs in concrete construction when elements of different mass are all monolithically produced. As the temperature changes, the thinner parts tend to cool down or warm up more rapidly than the thicker ones, since it takes longer for the interior mass of the thicker elements to feel the effect of temperature change. The result is that the movement of the thinner parts tends to be restrained by the thicker parts, inducing stresses in both parts. These stresses are usually most critical in the thinner parts and at the joints between the parts.

Another problem of differential thermal movements occurs between the exterior skin of the building and the interior mass. As shown in Figure 3.43, the exposed skin and any exposed structural elements in a multistoried building will move in

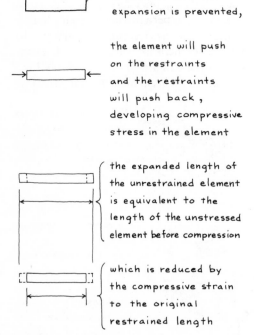

if a solid element is heated and its expansion is prevented,

the element will push on the restraints and the restraints will push back, developing compressive stress in the element

the expanded length of the unrestrained element is equivalent to the length of the unstressed element before compression

which is reduced by the compressive strain to the original restrained length

Figure 3.41 Effect of thermal change on a constrained element.

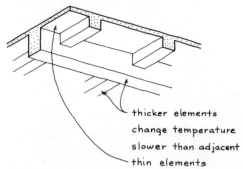

thicker elements change temperature slower than adjacent thin elements

Figure 3.42 Critical stress effects resulting from differential thermal movements.

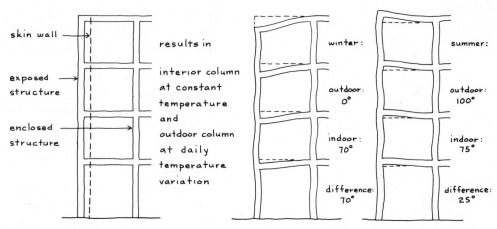

Figure 3.43 Effect of exposure conditions on development of thermally induced stress and strain.

response to the changes in outdoor temperature, while the interior elements of the building construction tend to remain at a relatively constant temperature, since the building interior is maintained at some comfort level for the occupants. This effect accumulates toward the top of the building and can result in major distortions in the upper portions of the structure.

When a building is long in plan dimension, a similar problem occurs when the exposed part of the building moves with respect to the interior part or the part that is buried in the ground. As shown in Figure 3.44, the ground temperature tends to remain constant throughout the year, and the effect is similar to that of the constant temperature of the building interior.

The degree of concern for these problems and the means for dealing with them

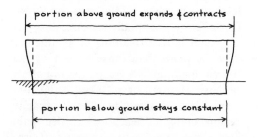

Figure 3.44 Thermal effects in partly submerged buildings.

vary, depending on the climate and the materials and details of the building construction. In some cases it is necessary to absorb the induced stresses in the building structure. In other cases it is possible to alleviate the problem by using expansion control joints, flexible connections, and so on, to hold the accumulative movements to a minimum or to prevent the transfer of stresses between adjacent parts of the construction.

3.4.4 Composite Structures

When materials or elements of different stiffness share a load, they develop resistances proportionate to their individual stiffnesses. As shown in Figure 3.45, if a group of springs share a load that shortens all of the springs the same amount, the amount of load taken by the stiffer springs will be greater, since it requires a greater effort to shorten them.

A common situation of this type occurs when concrete is reinforced with steel rods. When a load is applied to such an element resulting in the same amount of strain (shortening) of the concrete and steel, the steel will carry a percentage of the load disproportionate to its mass, since it is considerably stiffer than the concrete. Thus

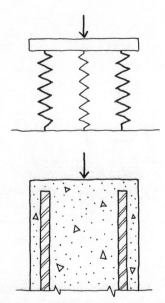

Figure 3.45 Load sharing in composite structures.

a relatively small percentage of steel in the cross section may carry a major portion of the load, since the elastic modulus for the steel can be 15 times or more than that of the concrete.

Another situation of this type occurs when elements of different construction share loads on the building. Figure 3.46 shows two examples of this situation. In the first example a masonry wall and a wood-framed wall occur on the same plane and share loads from the horizontal effects of wind or earthquakes. If the two walls are

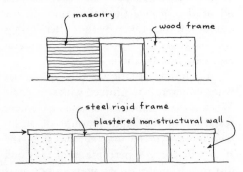

Figure 3.46 Load sharing by elements of different construction.

deformed the same amount—being held together by the wall construction between them and by the roof—the stiffer masonry wall will tend to take a greater portion of the load. If the difference in stiffness is great, it is common to ignore the resistance offered by the less stiff wall and to design the stiffer one to take the entire load. However, the effects of the dimensional distortion on the entire construction must be considered.

In the second example in Figure 3.46 the load is shared by a so-called rigid frame of steel and lightly framed walls with plastered surfaces. The plastered walls are likely to be much stiffer than the steel frame. The steel frame can tolerate considerable distortion, whereas the plaster will crack with a very small amount of distortion. The load at first will be taken by the stiffer plaster elements. Only after the plaster cracks will the steel frame deform sufficiently to absorb the load. While the best design solution simply may be to avoid such situations, it is also possible to assure that the load bypasses the plaster and is applied essentially to the frame. One way to achieve this is to provide relatively closely spaced control joints in the plastered surface that virtually constitute a sort of precracked condition.

3.4.5 Time-Related Stress and Strain

Some stress and strain phenomena are time related. Concrete is subject to an effect called creep (Figure 3.47), in which the material sustains a continuous, progressive deformation while held at constant stress. This effect is eventually self-arresting but can result in deformations of as much as twice or more than those caused by the original loading. The creep does not affect the basic strength or stiffness of the concrete. Thus its stress resistance capacity remains undiminished, and, if loaded again after some time, it will follow a stress–strain curve similar to its original one. There will, however, be some permanent,

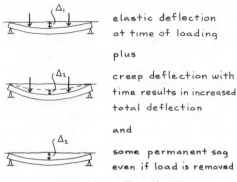

elastic deflection
at time of loading

plus

creep deflection with
time results in increased
total deflection

and

some permanent sag
even if load is removed

Figure 3.47 Effect of creep.

residual deformation, equal to that caused by the creep effect.

Creep does cause some redistribution of stresses between the concrete and steel in elements of reinforced concrete. Since the steel does not creep, it offers some resistance to the creep deformation of the adjacent concrete. This causes some additional shift of the share of load to the steel as the creep develops over time.

Soft, wet clay soils are subject to a time-related flow effect, similar to the slow oozing of toothpaste from a tube as a constant squeezing is maintained. If the soil mass is well constrained (as when the toothpaste cap is put back on) this effect can be self-arresting. However, as long as there is someplace for the clay to ooze toward, the flow will continue. Instances of

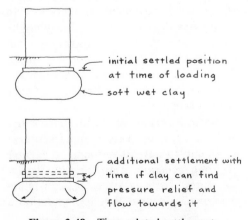

initial settled position
at time of loading
soft wet clay

additional settlement with
time if clay can find
pressure relief and
flow towards it

Figure 3.48 Time-related settlement.

buildings that continue to settle over many years have occurred with this soil condition (see Figure 3.48).

Another time-related stress problem occurs when elements are repeatedly loaded and unloaded. The repeated effect of people walking on stairs, wind rocking towers, or machinery shaking its structural supports are cases of this load condition in buildings. Some materials may fail from the fatigue effects of such loading. However, the problem is more often the loosening of connections or progressive development of cracks caused by other sources.

3.5 DYNAMIC EFFECTS

Vibrations, moving loads, and sudden changes in the state of motion, such as the jolt of rapid braking or acceleration, cause forces that result in stresses and strains in structures. The study of dynamic forces and their effects is very complex, although a few of the basic concepts can be illustrated simply.

For structural analysis and design the significant distinction between static and dynamic effects has to do with the response of the structure to the loading. If the principal response of the structure can be effectively evaluated in static terms (force, stress, linear deformation, etc.), the effect on the structure is essentially static, even though the load may be time-dependent in nature. If, however, the structure's response can be evaluated effectively only in terms of energy capacity, work accomplished, cyclic movements, and so on, the effect of the loading is of a true dynamic character.

A critical factor in the evaluation of the structure's response to dynamic loads is the fundamental time period of the structure's vibration. This is the time required for one full cycle of motion, in the form of a bounce or a continuing vibration. The relation of this time to the time of buildup of the load is a major factor in determining the relative degree of the dynamic effect on the structure. This period may vary from a fraction of a second to several seconds, depending on the size, mass, material, stiffness, support constraints, and possible presence of various damping effects on the structure's motion.

In the example in Figure 3.49 a single blow of the hammer causes the board to bounce in a vibratory manner described by the time–motion graph. The elapsed time for one full cycle of this motion is the fundamental period of vibration for the board. If a 100 lb load is applied at the end of the board by slowly and carefully stacking bricks on it, the load effect on the board is essentially static. However, if a 100 lb boy jumps on the end of the board, he will cause both an increase in deflection and a continued bouncing of the board, both of which are dynamic effects.

If the boy bounces on the end of the board with a particular rhythm, he can cause an extreme up and down motion of the board. He can find the rate of bounce required to do this easily by experimenting with different rhythms. He may also find the exact variation in his bouncing that will

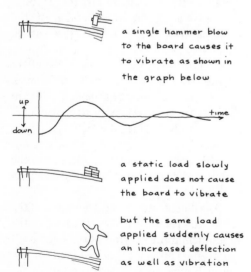

a single hammer blow to the board causes it to vibrate as shown in the graph below

a static load slowly applied does not cause the board to vibrate

but the same load applied suddenly causes an increased deflection as well as vibration

Figure 3.49 Dynamic effects on elastic structures.

result in an almost complete, instantaneous stop of the board's motion. As shown in the graph in Figure 3.50, the reinforcing bouncing that causes extreme motion of the board corresponds to the board's fundamental period. Thus at the end of each of these periods the board is traveling down, and the additional loading will increase this downward momentum. To stop the board the boy merely cuts the time of his bounce in half and meets the board on its way up; the two opposed motions collide to cancel each other's momentum.

If the boy bounces once on the board and then jumps off, the board will continue to bounce in ever-decreasing magnitudes of displacement until it eventually comes to rest. This deterioration of the board's motion is called damping. It occurs because of the energy dissipated in the springs or cushion mounts, in air friction, and other actions that use up some of the energy of the board's momentum. If the damping effects were not present, the repeated bouncing by the boy could result in a buildup of the board's displacement until damage occured.

Dynamic forces on structures result from a variety of natural and human-created sources. The actions of slapping waves, gusts of wind, earth tremors, moving vehicles, and falling objects are all potential sources of dynamic loads. Any of these can be damaging in terms of the total energy delivered to the structure or in terms of excessive movement or vibration. In some cases the structure itself may not be damaged, but the movements may result in the loosening of structural connections, in the shaking loose of objects attached to the structure, or in the discomfort of or injury to the occupants.

Natural periods of vibration for entire building structures vary from a fraction of a second to several seconds, the latter occuring generally only for tall, slender structures. Parts of structures can retain their own individual periods of vibration: a

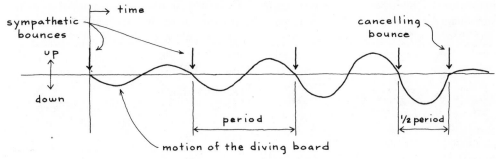

Figure 3.50 Motion of the diving board.

single span of a floor system may be bouncy when walked on while the rest of the structure is relatively unaffected.

Some dynamic effects can be reduced or eliminated by providing isolation or damping. Some damping occurs naturally as a result of the structure's stiffness or mass or its relative inefficiency in motion. Nonstructural parts of the building construction such as wall finishes, flooring, ceilings, and partitions are also sources of damping effects. Isolation can be achieved by separating vibration sources from the structure or by separating some parts of the structure from others. Vibration of heavy machinery is usually isolated partially from the structure by use of some sort of energy-absorbing mounting. Acoustic vibration of one surface of a wall can be isolated from the opposite surface by attaching one of the surfaces with energy-absorbing connectors or by providing each surface with its own independent structure.

Another type of vibration control is achieved by the use of a resonator—that is, a neutral element attached to the structure that can move independently. The motion of the resonator is tuned to the natural vibration of the structure in a way that makes it absorb or oppose the structure's free vibration.

Design for dynamic effects usually begins with an evaluation of the sources of dynamic loads and their potential effects on the structure. The response of the structure is then considered, using the variables of its mass, natural frequencies, energy-absorbing capabilities, natural damping, and so on. Once the dynamic behavior is understood, the designer can consider how to manipulate the variables to improve the structure's behavior or to reduce the load condition.

Several factors make design for dynamic effects difficult. One of these is the complex nature of a complete building structure's responses to dynamic loads and the resulting difficulty of quantifying these responses effectively. The mathematical complexity of dynamic analysis is considerably greater than that required for simple static effects. Consequently, most routine design for dynamic loads is done by translating the dynamic effects into equivalent static effects so that they can be dealt with by simpler and more familiar techniques.

Another difficulty with dynamic analysis is the somewhat subjective nature of some of the performance criteria. How much vibration is tolerable? How bouncy may a floor be? Judgments are often quite arbitrary, and there is considerable reliance on precedent and experience.

Design for earthquake effects is a major subject of dynamic analysis. There is much ongoing study and research in this area that results in continuing modification of codes and design standards. With the widespread use of computers, increasing use is being made of real dynamic analysis in design for earthquakes in place of the traditional simplified methods of equivalent static effects.

3.6   DESIGN FOR STRUCTURAL BEHAVIOR

In current professional structural design practice the investigation of structural behavior is an important part of the design process. To incorporate this investigation into the design work the designer needs to develop a number of capabilities, including the following:

1   The ability to visualize and evaluate the sources that produce loads on the structure.
2   The ability to quantify the loads and the effects they produce on the structure.
3   The ability to analyze the structure's response to the loads in terms of internal forces and stresses and strains.
4   The ability to evaluate the structure's limits of load-carrying capacity.
5   The ability to manipulate the variables of material, form, and construction details for the structure in order to optimize its responses to the loads.

Although analysis of stresses and strains is necessary in the design process, there is a sort of chicken and egg relationship between analysis and design. To analyze the structure's responses you need to know some of its properties, but to determine the necessary properties you need the results of the analysis. In simple cases it is sometimes possible to derive expressions for desired properties by the simple inversion or reversal of analytical formulas. For example, in a simple compression member, if the load produces a uniform stress on the cross section, the formula for this simple stress is

$$\text{stress} = \frac{\text{the total load on the member}}{\text{the area of the cross section}}$$

Therefore, if the load is known and the stress limit for the material is established, this formula is easily converted to one for finding the required area of the cross section, as follows:

$$\text{required area} = \frac{\text{the total load on the member}}{\text{the stress limit for the material}}$$

Most structural situations are more complex, however, and involve variables and relationships that are not so simply converted for design use. In the case of the compression member, for instance, if the member is a slender column the load capacity will be limited to some degree by the tendency to buckle, as discussed in the section on stability. The relative stiffness of the member in resisting buckling can be determined only after the geometry of the cross section is known. Therefore the design of such a structural element is a hit-or-miss proposition, consisting of guessing at an appropriate cross-sectional shape, analyzing for the load capacity, and refining as necessary until a reasonable relationship is established.

Professional designers use their own experience together with various design aids, such as tabulations of capacities of commonly used elements, to shortcut the design process. Detailed calculations for structural analysis are performed in many instances only after various shortcuts and approximations have been used to establish a preliminary design of the structure.

For any major structure it is necessary to perform a large number of calculations of stresses and load capacities in order to demonstrate the existence of an adequate load safety margin. Calculation of structural deformations is done less often, since the safety of the structure is seldom related to them. Only when the actual magnitudes of deformation are suspected to be of some detriment to the structure's use are these investigations made in the design process. An example of the latter is the deformation of flat-spanning elements, manifested as sag or deflection, which is quite often a critical design factor.

3.7 INVESTIGATION OF STRUCTURAL BEHAVIOR

Whether for design purposes, for research, or for the study of structural behavior as a learning experience, analysis of stresses and strains is important. Analysis may be performed as a testing procedure on the actual structure with a loading applied to simulate its actual usage conditions. If carefully done, this is a highly reliable procedure. However, except for some of the commonly used, simple elements of construction, it is generally not possible to perform destructive load testing on building structures built to full scale. Behavior of building structures must usually be anticipated speculatively on the basis of demonstrated performance of similar structures or on a modeling of the actions involved. This modeling can be done in the form of physical tests on scaled down structures, but is most often done mathematically, using the current state of knowledge in the form of formulas for analysis.

The body of knowledge used for the mathematical modeling of structural behavior is composed of the general areas of engineering science in applied mechanics, materials engineering, and structural engineering. Structural designers must be generally informed in these areas, and must develop a capability for using the various design aids and techniques for practical performance of design work. Considering the complexity of modern science and technology and the sophistication of modern computing techniques, this preparation is a major undertaking, generally achieved by the several years of study required for a graduate degree in engineering plus some apprenticeship in professional design work.

CHAPTER FOUR

Structural Materials

All materials—solid, liquid, or gaseous—
have some structural nature. The air we
breathe has a structural nature: it resists
compression. Every time you ride in an
automobile you are sitting on an air-
supported structure. Water supports the
largest human made vehicles: huge ocean
liners and battleships. Oil resists compression so strongly that it is used as the
resisting element in hydraulic presses and
jacks capable of developing tremendous
force.

In the design of building structures, use
is made of the available structural materials and the products formed from them.
The discussion in this chapter deals with
some of the basic materials themselves and
with their typical uses in contemporary
construction.

4.1 GENERAL CONSIDERATIONS

Broad classifications of materials can be
made such as distinctions between animal,
vegetable, and mineral; between organic
and inorganic materials; and between the
physical states of solid, liquid, and gaseous.
Various chemical and physical properties
distinguish individual materials from others. In studying or designing structures,
particular properties of materials are of
concern. These properties may be split
between essential structural properties and
general properties.

Essential structural properties of concern include the following:

Strength May vary for different types of
force, in different directions, at different
age or temperature.

Strain Resistance Degree of rigidity, elasticity, ductility, time, and temperature
effects.

Hardness Resistance to surface indenta-
tion and scratching.

Fatigue Resistance Time loss of strength,
shape change with time, and progressive
fracture.

Uniformity of Physical Structure Grain
and knots in wood, cracks in concrete,
shear planes in stone, effects of crystalliza-
tion in metals.

General properties of interest in using
and evaluating structural materials include
the following:

Form Natural or reconstituted.

Weight Must carry itself as well as applied loads.

Fire Resistance Combustibility, conduc-
tivity, performance at high temperatures,
melting point.

Coefficient of Thermal Expansion In
evaluating movements of structure with
temperature changes.

Durability Resistance to weathering, rot,
insects, and wear.

Workability In producing, shaping, assembling, and altering.

Appearance Natural or finished.

Availability and Cost

A working knowledge of both the general and structural properties of materials is essential to anyone involved with the conception, detailing, or evaluation of structures.

Let us consider the various common materials used in building structures. Although one material at a time is discussed, no significance should be attached to the sequence. The building components and systems possible with the various materials are discussed separately.

4.2   WOOD

Technical innovations of recent times have extended some of the longstanding limitations of wood. Size and form limitations have been overcome by employing glue lamination to build up structural elements from small-dimensioned lumber (see Figure 4.1). Special fastening systems have made larger-scale structures possible through better jointing. Combustibility, rot, and insect infestation can be retarded by utilizing chemical impregnations. Treatment with steam or ammonia gas can render the wood flexible, allowing it to assume plastic forms.

Dimensional movements from changes in temperature or moisture remain a problem in wood. Fire resistance can be developed only to a degree. Although easily worked, wood elements are soft and readily damaged, thus damage due to handling and use is a problem.

Although hundreds of species exist, building structural use is primarily limited to certain softwoods: Douglas fir, southern pine, northern white pine, spruce, redwood, cedar, and hemlock. Local availability and cost are major factors in the selection of a particular species. Economy is achieved by using the lowest grade of material suitable for the work. (Grade is a function of the lack of knots and splits as well as of the particular grain characteristic of an individual piece.)

One technological process has produced a unique wood element: the plywood sheet. This element has had tremendous usage and, though in danger of obsolescense because of other evolving sheet materials, is now experiencing some imaginative exploitation in various composite wood–plywood components and systems (see Figure 4.2).

In the development of structural elements it is not always wise or possible to use a single material. Structural materials are often mixed, each performing its appropriate tasks, such as in reinforced concrete construction. Figure 4.3 shows a series of light, medium-span roof trusses that have wood top and bottom elements and steel zig-zag interior elements. Compare these with the all steel trusses of similar form shown in Figure 4.4.

Because of its availability, low cost, and simple working possibilities, wood is used extensively for secondary and temporary constructions—that is, for scaffolding, bracing, and forming. This extensive use may give the impression that it is the only valid use of the material. However, if correctly used, the material can have lasting qualities sufficient for most requirements in building, for instance, the houses of Cape Cod, the temples of the Orient, and the timber roof members in many European churches.

4.3   STEEL

Steel is used in a variety of types and forms in nearly every building constructed. From huge H-columns to the smallest nails and screws, steel is the most versatile of traditional structural materials. It is also the strongest, the most resistant to aging, and the most reliable in quality. Steel is a completely industrialized material and is thus subject to tight control of its content and the details of its fabrication. It has the further desirable qualities of being noncombustible, nonrotting, and dimension-

Figure 4.1 Thomas O. Freeman Library, Lake Forest College, Lake Forest, Illinois. Glued laminated wood ribs radiate from a central core in 20° increment spacing to form the roof of this small library. Roof deck is glued laminated wood hung in tension from the ribs. Architects: Perkins and Will, Chicago. Structural engineers: The Engineers Collaborative, Chicago. Photo: The Engineers Collaborative.

Figure 4.2 Plywood space planes. Prefabricated units of wood–plywood construction are assembled to form the folded plate roof of this church in St. Paul, Minnesota. Architects: Buetow Associates. Photo: American Plywood Association, Tacoma, Washington.

ally stable with time and moisture change (see Figure 4.4).

Although the bulk material itself is expensive, it can be used in small quantities because of its great strength and its forming processes, making it competitive with materials of lower bulk cost. Economy can also be achieved through mass production in its industrialized process.

Two principal disadvantages of steel for building structures are inherent in the material. These are its rapid heat gain and resultant loss of strength when exposed to the intense heat of a fire and its corrosion when exposed to moisture and air or corrosive conditions. Several techniques can be used to overcome its fire sensitivity,

including the use of special paints that expand in volume when heated, forming a noncombustible surface insulation. Coatings of one kind or another are also the best protection against corrosion, although some recently developed steels resist ordinary air rusting sufficiently to be left exposed without any treatment.

Figure 4.5 shows the use of a fire-resistive material for protecting steel. This material is sprayed on to the steel surfaces where it adheres and is built up to a thickness appropriate for the desired degree of insulation. Although somewhat messy, this material offers the advantage of easily covering complicated forms such as trusses and the undersides of formed sheet

Figure 4.3 Composite structural elements. Light trusses with wood top and bottom chords and steel web elements.

steel decks. If wall and ceiling construction covers the structure, the lack of visual delight is not a problem.

The vocabulary of steels in use for building structures has recently been expanded, and there is now a wide range from which to choose the correct steel for a particular situation of stress magnitude, corrosion, form of elements, or fastening technique. It is not uncommon for the various elements of the framework of a steel building to consist of a dozen or more varieties of material, with a wide spectrum of property variation. For example, the steel used in the wire of woven cable is five times as strong as that used for ordinary steel beams!

4.4   CONCRETE

In building construction, the word concrete is used to describe a variety of materials having one thing in common: the use of a binding agent to form a solid mass from a loose, inert aggregate. The three basic ingredients of ordinary concrete are water, a binding agent (such as cement), and a large volume of loose aggregate (such as sand and gravel). Tremendous variation of the endproduct is possible with the use of different binders and aggregate and with the use of special chemicals and air-void-producing foaming agents.

Ordinary Stone Concrete   This is the material of sidewalks, highway pavements, and foundations. The binder is Portland cement and the aggregate is sand and gravel. The resulting material is the familiar rocklike substance of high compressive resistance and considerable weight.

Structural Lightweight Concrete   This is the same as ordinary concrete, except that some special aggregate is used to replace the gravel. Various substitutes are slag, expanded shale, clinkers, and other substances that combine light weight with considerable strength. Weight reduction of up to one-third may be effected without loss of strength. There is, however, some unavoidable loss in stiffness. Higher cost of the special aggregate is usually offset by savings realized because of the reduced weight of the structure.

Figure 4.4 Steel building components. (*Upper*) Typical steel elements: rolled column and beams, light trussed open-web joists and corrugated deck. (*Lower*) Steel framework with infilling floor consisting of corrugated sheet steel and light-gage metal ducts for electrical distribution. (Floor units are Cofar and Cel-Way by Granco Steel Products Company, St. Louis, Missouri.) Photo: Granco Steel Products.

Insulating Lightweight Concrete Use of an even lighter aggregate—such as a mineral substance popped like popcorn—plus a foaming agent to produce air voids can produce a material as light as one-fifth that of ordinary stone gravel concrete. Loss of strength is unavoidable—usually roughly proportional to the weight reduction. This material is widely used as insulating fill on light steel corrugated deck and as a fireproofing material for steel frame members.

Gypsum Concrete This is similar to insulating lightweight concrete except that the binder consists of gypsum. The common aggregate used is wood chip. Uses are similar to those of lightweight insulating concrete.

Figure 4.5 Sprayed-on fireproofing material applied to steel beams and the underside of a steel deck.

High Early Strength Concrete Concrete made with special cement having an accelerated strength gain, making it usable in one-quarter the usual time.

White Concrete The use of special white cement, white sand, and aggregate, and virtually antiseptic mixing and forming equipment can result in a sparkling white product, in contrast to the normal dull grey-green color.

Expansive Concrete Some use is made of chemically altered cement that produces a slight expansion of the mass during curing. This may be used to neutralize the normal volume loss due to shrinkage, or even to reverse it. The latter use is the basis for the so-called self-prestressing concrete. A principal advantage is in the elimination of cracking caused by normal shrinkage.

Ordinary concrete has several attributes, chief among which are its low bulk cost and its resistance to moisture, rot, insects, fire, and wear. Since it is formless in its mixed condition, it can be made to assume a large variety of forms. Large-scale, monolithic structures are naturally formed with this material (see Figure 4.6).

One of concrete's chief shortcomings is its lack of tensile stress resistance. The use of inert or prestressed reinforcing is imperative for any structural function involving considerable bending or torsion. Precisely because the material is formless, its forming and finishing is often one of the major expenses in its use. Factory precasting in permanent forms is one current technique used to overcome this problem (see Figure 4.7).

4.5 ALUMINUM

In alloyed form, aluminum is used for a large variety of structural, decorative, and functional elements in building construction. Principal advantages are its light

Figure 4.6 Temple Street parking garage, New Haven, Connecticut. Reinforced concrete frame detailed to express the natural form of a structure of monolithic material. Surface texture is produced by careful detailing of the wooden forms. Architect: Paul Rudolph. Structural engineer: Henry A. Pfisterer.

weight (one-third that of steel) and its high resistance to corrosion. Among the disadvantages are its softness, its low stiffness, its high rate of thermal expansion, its lower resistance to fire, and its relatively high cost (see Figure 4.8).

Large-scale structural use in buildings is limited primarily because of cost or increased dimensional movements caused by the low stiffness of the material. This low stiffness also reduces its resistance to buckling. Small-scale structural use—wall and roof skin panels, door and window frames, and hardware—is considerable, however. Here its corrosion resistance, easy working character, and the possibilities for its forming in production are at best advantage.

4.6 MASONRY

This term is used to describe a variety of formations consisting of separate elements bonded together by some binding filler. The elements may be cut or rough stone, fired clay tile or bricks, or cast units of concrete. The binder is traditionally cement–lime mortar, although considerable

effort is being made in experimentation with various new adhesive compounds. The resulting assemblage is similar to a concrete structure and possesses many of the same properties. A major difference is that the construction process does not usually require the same amount of temporary forming and bracing as it does for a structure of poured concrete. However, it requires considerable hand labor, which imposes some time limitations and makes the endproduct highly subject to the individual skill of the craftsperson.

Reinforcing techniques have been developed in recent years to extend the structural possibilities of masonry. Figure 4.9 shows a typical form of construction currently in wide use in the western United States because of its significantly improved resistance to earthquakes.

Shrinkage of the mortar and thermal-expansion cracking are two major problems with masonry structure. Both necessitate extreme care in detailing, material quality control, and field inspection during construction.

4.7 PLASTICS

Plastic elements represent the widest variety of usage in building construction. The tremendous variation of material properties and formation processes provides a virtually unlimited field for the designer's imagination. Some of the principal problems with plastics are lack of fire resistance, low stiffness, high rate of thermal expansion, and some cases of chemical or physical instability with time.

Use of these materials advances steadily as they replace more traditional materials and also create entirely new functional possibilities. A few of the more important uses in building construction are:

Glass Substitute In clear or translucent form, as bubble-form skylights, window panes, and corrugated sheet panels (see Figures 4.10, 5.23, and 5.33).

Figure 4.7 Precast concrete building elements. Large-scale factory-produced concrete elements have given a new dimension to this traditional material. Accuracy of detail and quality of finish attained exceed those possible for poured-in-place construction. (*Upper*) Two-story-high exterior wall units form the shell of this building, supported by a large unique concrete platform with only four supports. Glendale Municipal Services Building, Glendale, California. Architects: Albert C. Martin and Associates, Los Angeles. (*Lower*) The exterior wall structure of this high-rise building consists of hollow, precast concrete units filled with poured concrete during the construction of the poured-in-place floor structure. This technique preserves many of the best qualities of both precast and poured-in-place, monolithic construction. Beneficial Standard Life Insurance Company Building, Los Angeles, California. Architects: Skidmore, Owings and Merrill, San Francisco. Precast units by Rockwin Schokbeton, Santa Fe Springs, California.

Figure 4.8 Aluminum geodesic dome. This 144-ft diameter dome was the first of its type produced by Kaiser Aluminum and Chemical Sales, Inc. The dome consists of 575 preformed, diamond-shaped panels of thin aluminum sheets. The panels were completely erected, using a central rigging mast, in 20 working hours. Cast aluminum gussets serve the dual purposes of connecting the six panels that meet at a joint and facilitating attachment of the rigging cables. Architects: Welton Becket and Edwin L. Bauer (for the first dome—a 2000-seat auditorium for the Hawaiian Village Hotel in Honolulu). Geodesic system patented by R. Buckminster Fuller. Photos by Werner Stoy, Honolulu, Hawaii; supplied by Kaiser Aluminum and Chemical Sales, Inc., Oakland, California.

Coatings Sprayed, painted, or rolled in liquid form, or layed on in films or sheets to provide protection for walls, roofs, foundation walls, and counter tops.

Adhesives The famous epoxy family of bonding and matrix binders for connecting and patching.

Formed Elements Mouldings, fixtures, panels, and hardware.

Foamed In preformed or foamed-in-place applications, as insulation and filler for various purposes.

The development in recent years of air-inflated and tension-sustained membrane structures has spurred the development of various plastic membrane and fabric products for building use. Figure 4.11 shows a simple structure consisting essentially only of a thin plastic membrane. For larger-scale structures, the surface material usually consists of a reinforced fabric for greater strength (see Figure 5.30).

The plastic-surfaced structure can also be created by using plastic elements on a framework. A special variation of this is the steel cable structure that uses the cables to define a network and then uses translucent plastic elements to form the surface (see Figure 5.27).

The use of plastics for building structures is still inhibited by the traditional conservatism of building regulatory agencies, by the largely unwarranted associations of cheapness and impermanence in the minds of architects, engineers, and public, by the oil shortage, and by increasing concern for the performance of plastics during fires. However, evolution of taste, custom, and design standards and the expansion of the technology will inevitably encourage its increased use. Figure 4.12 shows a prototype shell structure for a house that was developed in the early 1950s.

Figure 4.9   Reinforced masonry construction. Steel reinforcing rods are placed both vertically and horizontally in the hollow voids and grout is placed around the rods, filling the voids. The result is in effect similar to the creation of a two-way rigid frame of reinforced concrete inside the wall.

4.8   SOIL

Although soil is not used often as an actual building material, it is nevertheless very much in use structurally in a variety of ways. As a foundation material, its compressive resistance in terms of strength and dimensional compaction are extremely important. As the direct support of floor and paving slabs, it is really *the* structure in these cases. In the construction of terraces, berms and earth dams, it may serve the functions of space definition and retaining.

Construction in, on, and with soil is a whole field in itself. Chief aspects of relevance to building design are the determination of the basic type of foundation and its specific load limits, the orientation of the structure to special features of the topology and geological configuration of the site and its substructure, water conditions, evaluation of surface soils as support for pavements, and the special provisions necessary to perform the excavation for construction.

4.9   MISCELLANEOUS MATERIALS

Glass   Ordinary glass possesses considerable strength, but has the undesirable characteristic of being brittle and subject to shattering under shock. Special treatment can increase its strength and shock resistance, but it is relatively expensive for use in large quantities. Large-scale structural use is not conceivable for this material. Considerable use is made, however, for surfacing panels as well as transparent window panes.

Figure 4.10 Domed plastic skylights. 180 bubble-shaped skylights in metal frames form the roof for this swimming pool at the Ambassador Motor Lodge in Minneapolis, Minnesota. The individual bubbles of Plexiglas are 90 in. square in plan. Designers: Synergetics, Inc., Raleigh, North Carolina. Photos: Rohm and Haas Company, Philadelphia.

Figure 4.11 Air-supported structure. Vinyl plastic sheets of 20-gage thickness with seams cold-bonded by chemical solvent form this classically simple, highly functional pool cover. Stability is maintained by a small air compressor that produces an internal air pressure of from 2 to $2\frac{1}{2}$ lb/ft^2. A simple zippered entrance plus a water-filled base edge are the only details required. Micolite Industries of California, Van Nuys, California.

Figure 4.12 The Monsanto "House of the Future" at Disneyland in Anaheim, California. Molded plastic modules reinforced with glass fiber form the roof, floors, and walls of this experimental house that opened for display in June 1957. Developed by Monsanto Chemical Co. in cooperation with architects Hamilton and Goody of Cambridge, Massachusetts, following preliminary design and research at the Massachusetts Institute of Technology. Lower photo shows a cutaway section of the floor structure.

Figure 4.13 Typical example of use of multiple materials for a single building structure. Shown here: concrete floor slab and foundations, reinforced masonry walls, steel columns, wood beams and plywood, composite wood and steel trusses.

Fiber Glass A special use of glass is made by producing it in fibrous form, in which it is capable of realizing close to its ideal strength. This strength may exceed that of high-strength steel, and although its form restricts its usage, various structural utilizations can be achieved. One familiar use is that in which the fibers are suspended in a resin, producing fiber glass reinforced plastic.

Paper Paper—that is, sheet material of basically rag or wood fiber content—is used considerably in building construction. It has been replaced in many uses, however, by sheet plastic. Various coatings, laminations, impregnations, and reinforcings can be used to make the material water resistant, rot resistant, or tougher. Structural use, however, is limited to relatively minor functions, one being a forming material for poured concrete. Paper-faced plaster panels are used in "drywall."

The most ordinary of buildings will typically use a great number of different materials in its construction (see Figure 4.13). A building structure is usually composed of some elements of all the basic materials. Wood and steel framed structures have concrete foundations; concrete and masonry structures use steel reinforcing; wood structures use a great many steel fastening devices; and so on. Structural design typically consists of matching choices from an almost endless number of possible combinations.

An exhaustive list of structural materials for building would include many more types than those mentioned. I have only described the major ones and a few minor ones. Continuous expansion of our technology and experimentation by designers increases the number of materials as well as the variety of uses of the established materials.

CHAPTER FIVE

Structural Systems

The materials, products, and systems available for the construction of building structures constitute a vast inventory through which the designer must sift carefully for the appropriate selection in each case. The material in this chapter presents some of the general issues relating to this inventory.

5.1 ATTRIBUTES OF STRUCTURAL SYSTEMS

A specific structural system derives its unique character from any of a number of considerations—most likely from many of them simultaneously. Separately considered, these are the following:

1 Specific structural functions, some of which are support in compression (a pier, footing, or column); support in tension (a straight vertical hanger or a guy wire); spanning—horizontally (a beam in a floor), vertically (a sheet of window glass), or in some other position (a sloping rafter); cantilevering—vertically (a flagpole or tower) or horizontally (a balcony or canopy). A single element or system may be required to perform more than one of these functions in various situations of use.

2 The geometric form or orientation. Note the difference between the nature of the flat beam and the arch, both of which function as horizontally spanning structures. The difference is primarily one of overall structural form. Compare the arch with the draped cable, both in use as horizontally spanning elements. They are obviously different in function. The difference, however, is not one of form but of orientation to the load.

3 The material(s) of the elements.

4 The manner of joining the elements if the system consists of an articulated set of parts.

5 The manner of supporting the structure.

6 The specific loading conditions, or the forces the structure must sustain.

7 The separately imposed considerations of usage in terms of form and scale limits.

8 The limitations of form and scale of the elements and the nature of their joining imposed by the properties of the materials, the production processes, and the need for special functions such as demountability and movement.

Structural systems occur in virtually endless variety. The designer, in attempting to find the ideal structure for a specific purpose, is faced with an exhaustive process of comparative "shopping." Most designers agree that, except for a few special situations, there is no such thing as the ideal structure for any particular job. At best, the shopping can narrow the field to a few acceptable solutions.

Figure 5.1 Santa Ines Mission Church, Santa Ynez Valley, California. Historical craft-developed building techniques are illustrated in this structure, built in the early part of the last century. Huge buttresses of adobe and brick brace the walls of the church—a reaction to the destruction of an earlier church by an earthquake. Hand-hewn wood beams and planks form the roof of the arcade, supported on one side by a series of brick arches. Although these forms and techniques are the endproducts of a long development of building tradition and still in effect valid, they have been made largely obsolete by our contemporary industrialized technology.

A checklist of sorts can be used to rate the available systems for a given purpose. The following are some items that may be included in such a list:

Economy The economy of the structure itself as well as its influence on the overall economy of the project. Special consideration may be given factors such as delay because of slow construction, adaptability to modifications, and first cost versus maintenance cost over the life of the structure.

Special Structural Requirements Unique aspects of the structure's action, details required for development of its strength and stability, adaptability to special loading, need for symmetry or modular arrangement. Thus arches require horizontal resisting forces at their bases to resist their thrusts, tension elements must be hung *from* something, structures of thin metal parts must be stiffened for stability against buckling, and domes must have some degree of symmetry and a concentric continuity.

Problems of Design Difficulty of performing an analysis of the structural action, ease of detailing the structure, ease of integrating the physical structure with the detail requirements of its use.

Problems of Construction Availability of materials and of skilled labor and equipment, adaptability to unitized fabrication and assembly and to prefabrication, speed of erection, special requirements for temporary bracing or support, required skill and precision of field work.

Material and Scale Limitations The feasibility range of size for specific systems. These vary with the development of new materials and new techniques and with experimentation of new uses for existing systems. Though records are transient, certain practical limits do exist and, in many cases, are virtually insurmountable.

5.2 CATEGORIZATION OF STRUCTURAL SYSTEMS

Structural systems can be categorized in a variety of ways. One broad differentiation is that made between solid structures, framed structures, and surface structures.

Solid structures (Figure 5.2) are those in which strength and stability are achieved through mass, even though the structure is not completely solid. Large piers and abutments, dams, sea walls, retaining walls, caves, and ancient burial pyramids are examples. These structures are highly resistive to forces such as those created by blasts, violent winds, wave action, and vibrations. Although their exact analysis may be highly indeterminate, the distribution of load stresses may be diffuse enough to allow simple approximations with a reasonable assurance of safety.

In framed structures (Figure 5.3), the essential structure consists of a network of assembled elements. The building, bridge, or ship is completed by filling in the voids as required between these spaced elements. Even though the infilling elements may have a structural character themselves and serve to stiffen and brace the frame, they

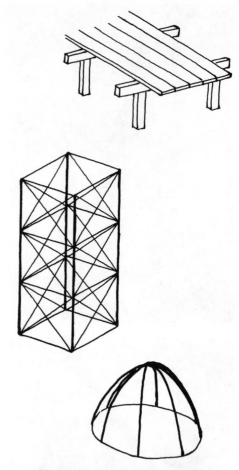

Figure 5.3 Framed structures.

are not primary elements of the basic structure. Animal skeletons, steel beam and column systems, and trussed towers are examples. These structures are generally most adaptable to variations in form, dissymmetry of layout or detail, and the carrying of special loads. They can be cumbersome, however, if the complexity of their assembly details becomes excessive. The attachment of the infilling elements must also be facilitated.

Surface structures (Figure 5.4) can be very efficient because of their simultaneous twofold function as structure and enclosure and because they may be inherently very stable and strong, especially in the case of three-dimensional forms. They are, how-

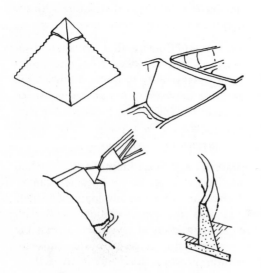

Figure 5.2 Solid structures.

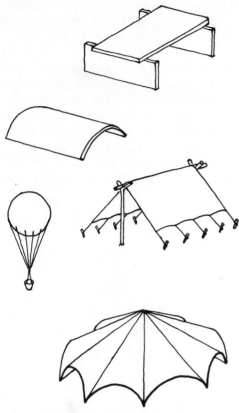

Figure 5.4 Surface structures.

systems and possibly even invent systems with no existing categorical identification.

A complete presentation of all conceivable structural materials and systems and a discussion of their relative merits, potentialities, and limitations would undoubtedly fill a volume several times the size of this book. Indeed it may require several volumes. Nevertheless, a short survey of traditional systems with some commentary follows.

The categorization used—for example, post and beam and arch—has no particular preference or relative significance. It is merely a convenient one for discussion. It has an open end, since it does not preclude new categories.

5.3 STRUCTURAL WALLS

It seems to be a direct structural development to use the enclosing and dividing walls of a building for support and bracing. When this system is utilized there are usually two distinct elements in the total building structure:

The Walls Used to provide lateral stability as well as to support the spanning elements.

Spanning Elements Function as floors or roofs.

ever, somewhat limited in resisting concentrated loads and in facilitating sudden discontinuities such as openings. Furthermore, the mathematics of their analysis can be extremely complicated.

Other categorizations can be made for particular types of construction or configuration of the structure. Thus we describe certain family groups such as structural walls, post and beam, arch, suspension, pneumatic, trussed, folded plate, or thin shell systems. Each of these has certain characteristics and is subject to specific material–scale limitations. Each lends itself most aptly to certain uses. A knowledge of the specific attributes of the various systems is essential to the designer but can be gained only by exhaustive study and some experience. The inventive designer can, of course, consider new variations of the basic

The spanning elements are usually structurally distinct from the walls and can be considered separately. They may consist of a variety of assemblies, from simple wooden boards and joists to complex precast concrete or steel truss units. The flat spanning system is discussed as a separate category.

Bearing walls are essentially compression elements. They may be monolithic, or they may be frameworks assembled of many pieces. They may be uninterrupted, or they may be pierced in a variety of ways (see Figure 5.5). Holes for windows and

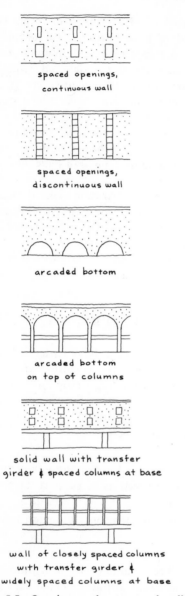

spaced openings,
continuous wall

spaced openings,
discontinuous wall

arcaded bottom

arcaded bottom
on top of columns

solid wall with transfer
girder & spaced columns at base

wall of closely spaced columns
with transfer girder &
widely spaced columns at base

Figure 5.5 Opening up the structural wall.

doors may be punched in the solid wall, and, as long as their heads are framed and they are arranged so as not to destroy the structural potential of the wall, the structure remains intact.

A special case of the pierced wall is the arcaded bottom. This is a wall whose base is opened up a considerable degree by a series of arches. The arches are placed very close together, resulting in what is actually a transition from the solid wall to a series of spaced piers, or columns. Different in structural character but similar in form is the structure in which a heavy beam is used at the base of the wall and is supported by a series of spaced columns.

A fine line of distinction exists between a framed bearing wall and a skin wall applied to a structural frame (Figure 5.6). Consider the traditional wood stud wall, consisting of wood two-by-fours on 16 in.

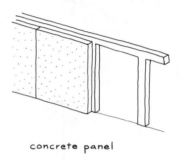

concrete panel

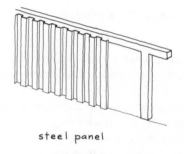

steel panel

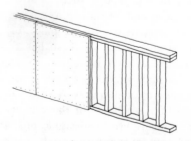

plywood sheathing on wood studs

Figure 5.6 Framed walls with infill.

centers to which two surfaces are attached.
These surfaces may be lath and plaster,
wood boards and siding, plywood sheets,
or gypsum drywall panels. While this structure is a framework initially—the two-by-
fours alone—it becomes a monolithic, rigid
wall when surfaces are attached. The surfaces will unavoidably interact with the
two-by-fours, especially in resisting lateral
force in the plane of the wall.

In contrast to the wood stud wall,
which is monolithic in character, consider
the cases of a steel frame to which a light
surface is attached. This surface may be,
for example, thin corrugated aluminum
sheets or light wood-framed window units.
If the steel frame is relatively rigid, the wall
surface probably has little interaction with
it, or at least contributes very little to the
overall structural resistance of the system.
In fact, to prevent damage to the surface
wall, the detailing of the assemblage may
deliberately eliminate load transfer between the frame and the wall. The deflection of a beam at the edge of a floor or roof,
for example, must not be restrained by the
wall unless the wall is capable of supporting
the beam.

Even though not used for vertical load
transfer, walls are often used to provide
lateral stability. This can be achieved by the
wall acting independently or in combined
interaction with the frame of the building.
An example of the latter is a plywood sheet
attached to a series of wooden studs. Even
if it does not share in vertical load development, it will function in preventing lateral
collapse of the studs. This lateral bracing
potential of the rigid vertical plane is often
utilized in stabilizing buildings against the
forces of wind or seismic shock.

Consider the simple structure shown in
Figure 5.7, which consists of a single space
bounded by four walls and a flat roof. The
two heavy vertical end walls in the upper
illustration are capable of resisting horizontal force in a direction parallel to the
plane of the walls. However, horizontal
forces in a direction perpendicular to the

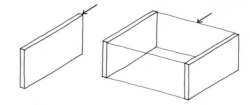

stable in one direction only

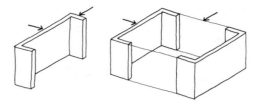

stable in both directions

Figure 5.7 Stability of walls.

plane of the walls would not be resisted as
easily. If the other two walls of the structure are also rigid, they may, of course,
function to resist horizontal forces parallel
to their planes, thus providing complete
support for the building. Another device,
however, is that of simply turning the two
end walls slightly around the corners, as
shown in the lower illustration. This makes
them independently stable against horizontal forces from all directions.

The device just illustrated is one technique for stabilizing the flat wall against
horizontal force perpendicular to its plane.
It may also be necessary to stabilize the
wall against buckling under vertical loads if
it is very tall and thin. In addition to folding
or curving the wall in plan, some other
means for achieving this transverse resistance are given below (see Figure 5.8).

Spreading the Base This can be done by
actually fattening the wall toward its base
as with a gravity dam or by attaching the
wall rigidly to a broad footing.

Stiffening the Wall with Ribs The wall
can be thickened locally, forming monolithic ribs, or pilasters, which also function
to receive concentrated vertical loads on
the wall.

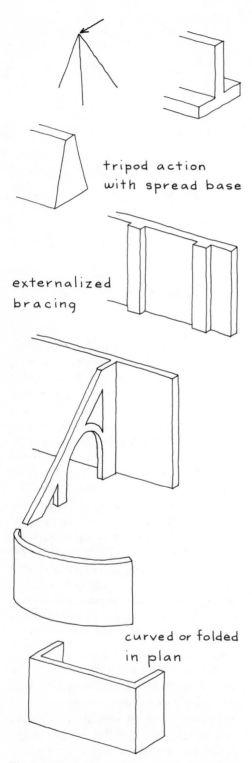

tripod action
with spread base

externalized
bracing

curved or folded
in plan

Figure 5.8 Various means of stabilizing walls.

Bracing the Wall External bracing devices such as buttresses, struts, and guys function strictly for lateral force resistance.

If the wall functions as a horizontal spanning element, as it does in the arcaded base structure, its basic structural behavior depends on the ratio of the span to the height of the wall. If this ratio is less than three or so, the wall does not act strictly as a beam but develops a corbeling or arching action depending on the construction and material of the wall. A horizontal lintel placed over an opening in a masonry wall does not actually support the entire wall directly over it but only some triangular portion immediately above it. If this triangular portion is eliminated, the form of the corbeled opening is anticipated, whereby the wall spans the opening effortlessly. If an arch is used for the top of the opening, it may actually function as little more than a liner for the opening.

Let us briefly consider the use of some of the traditional materials for structural walls.

Masonry The widest use of structural masonry walls is in units of precast concrete. Some use is also made of brick, tile, and composite brick–concrete block construction. Advances in the development of mortars, mortar-replacing adhesives, reinforcing techniques, expansion-joint materials, insulating and surface sealing materials, and prefabrication techniques keep this ancient construction system competitive with more recently developed building systems. Dependence on the skill of hand labor remains a problem. The qualities of solidity, apparent permanence, and durability make it appealing to the public. The sheer weight of the construction can be an advantage in providing stability and solidity but also adds to the weight that must be borne by the supporting structures and foundations.

Reinforced Concrete Since its rebirth in the middle of the last century, this material has steadily taken over many of the functions previously performed by masonry. Major expenses in the poured concrete wall are the forming and reinforcing required. No other material can achieve the degree of monolithicity and shear massiveness possible with this material.

The fairly recent widespread development of large-scale precast concrete structural elements has added a new dimension to uses of concrete. Other technological developments in the basic materials, the mixing and placing techniques, and special reinforcing by prestressing have broken old barriers of scale, form, detail, finish, and limits of the structural system.

Wood As a structural wall material, wood is largely limited to the stud wall and the plywood sheet. Wall surfacing of boards for the most part has been replaced by large-dimension sheets of plywood and fiberboard. Though wood is strong and tough, its lack of fire resistance and dimensional instability with moisture and temperature change are still drawbacks. Its relative cheapness and simplicity of handling make it highly competitive, however, wherever it is functionally sufficient. The aesthetic appeal of natural exposed wood is often a major factor in its preference.

Metal Steel frames with interactive infill panels or surfacing are increasingly used in the current trend toward the industrialization of the building process. Corrugated or pleated sheet metal or metal-faced sandwich panels with plastic cores are also in increasing use. Lack of dead weight can be advantageous but can also result in a lightness and flexibility that gives a feeling of flimsiness to the structure. A common system is the steel frame with masonry, precast concrete, or even poured concrete infilling walls. In the last named system the walls give lateral bracing to the frame and also add the desired degree of solidity to the structure.

Plastics Plastics currently enjoy their widest use in composite elements such as the metal-faced sandwich panel mentioned above. The same panel may, however, be plastic-faced. The potential for all plastic structural elements has not yet been extensively explored.

5.4 POST AND BEAM

Primitive cultures' use of tree trunks as building elements were the origin of this basic system. Later expansion of the vocabulary of materials into stone, masonry, concrete, and metals carried over the experience and tradition of form and detail established with wood. This same tradition, plus the real potentialities inherent in the system, keep this building technique a major part of our structural repertoire (see Figure 5.9).

The two basic elements of the system are the post and the beam (lintel):

Post Essentially a linear compression element subject to crushing or buckling, depending on its relative slenderness.

Beam (Lintel) Essentially a linear element subject to transverse load; must develop internal resistance to shear and bending and resist excessive deflection (sag).

Critical aspects of the system are the relation of length to radius of gyration (or simple thickness) of the post and the relation of depth to span of the beam. Efficiency of the geometric cross-sectional shape of the beam in bending resistance is also critical. (See the discussion of bending in Chapter 3.)

The stability of the system under lateral

Figure 5.9 Buena Park Civic Center, Buena Park, California. Self-stabilizing masonry columns and simply detailed wood framing produce a structure with a clear lineage of historical development. The parts of the structure, however, are quite evidently of contemporary industrial origin. Architects: Smith and Williams, South Pasadena, California.

loading is critical in two different ways (see Figure 5.10). Consider first the resistance to horizontal load in the same plane as the frame. This resistance can be provided in a number of ways, for instance, by fixing the base of the posts, using self-stabilizing posts, connecting the posts and beam rigidly (as in the legs of a table), using trussing or X-bracing, or by using a sufficiently rigid infilling panel.

Stability against horizontal loads perpendicular to the plane of the frame is a slightly different situation. Many of the same techniques of bracing can be used for this also. Another possibility is having an interaction between the frame and the infilling elements used to span from frame to frame, since the three-dimensional building usually implies a set, or series, of frames.

Some variations on the basic system are the following (see Figure 5.11).

Use of Extended Beam Ends   Produces overhangs, or cantilevers. This serves to reduce the degree of bending and sag at the center of the span, thus increasing the relative efficiency of the spanning element.

Rigid Attachment of Beam and Posts   A device for producing stability in the plane of the frame, as already discussed. It achieves some reduction of bending and sag at midspan of the beam, but does so at the expense of the post—in contrast to the extended beam ends. It also produces an outward kick at the base of the post.

Rigid Attachment with Extended Beam Ends   Combines the stabilizing advantage of the rigid attachment with the sag and bracing required for :

lateral force
in plane
of frame

lateral force
normal to
plane of frame

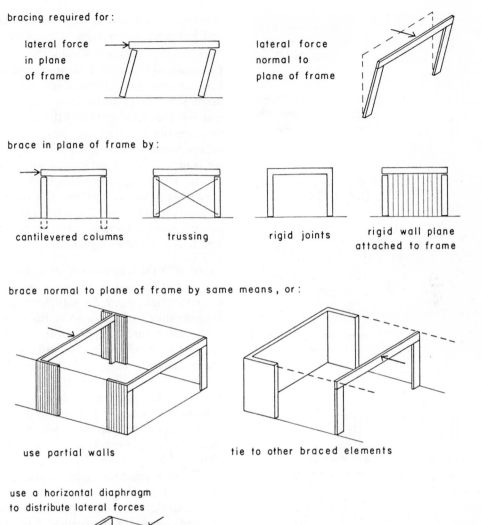

brace in plane of frame by :

cantilevered columns   trussing   rigid joints   rigid wall plane
                                                                        attached to frame

brace normal to plane of frame by same means , or :

use partial walls   tie to other braced elements

use a horizontal diaphragm
to distribute lateral forces

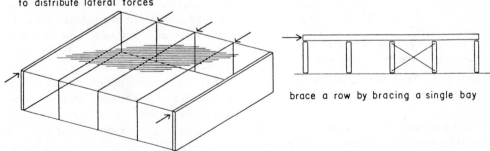

brace a row by bracing a single bay

Figure 5.10 Bracing of framed structures for lateral loads. (From *Simplified Building Design for Wind and Earthquake Forces*, James Ambrose and Dimitry Vergun, John Wiley & Sons, New York, 1980, with permission.)

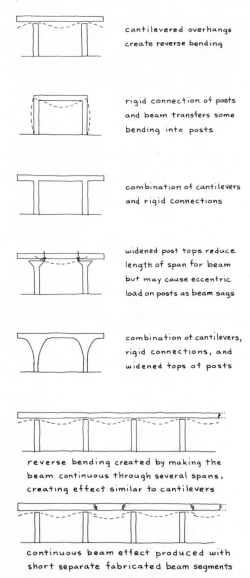

cantilevered overhangs create reverse bending

rigid connection of posts and beam transfers some bending into posts

combination of cantilevers and rigid connections

widened post tops reduce length of span for beam but may cause eccentric load on posts as beam sags

combination of cantilevers, rigid connections, and widened tops of posts

reverse bending created by making the beam continuous through several spans, creating effect similar to cantilevers

continuous beam effect produced with short separate fabricated beam segments

Figure 5.11 Variations of the post and beam.

bending reduction of the extended ends. If carefully designed, the bending in the posts and kick at the base can be eliminated.

Widened Top of Post Serves to reduce the span of the beam. As the beam deflects and curves, however, its load becomes concentrated at the edge of the top of the post, thus causing bending in the post. Several variations are possible using, for example, V-shaped or Y-shaped posts.

Widened Post Top with Rigid Attachment and Extended Beam Ends Can combine advantages of all three techniques.

Continuous (Monolithic, Multispan) Beam Produces the same effects as the extended beam ends for the single span. Additional gain is in the tying together of the system. A variation in which internal joints are placed off the column preserves the advantages of the bending and sag reductions but allows shorter beam segments. This latter is an advantage in wood, steel, and precast concrete structures. Poured-in-place concrete can, of course, achieve virtually any desired length of monolithic structure.

As with the wall-bearing structure, the post and beam requires the use of a secondary structural system for infilling to produce the solid surfaces of walls, floors, and roofs (see Figure 5.12). A great variety is possible in these systems, as discussed in the section on walls and flat spanning systems. One possible variation is to combine the post and wall monolithically, producing a series of pilasters. Similarly, the beam and flat deck may be combined monolithically, producing a continuous ribbed deck or a series of T-shaped beams.

The post and beam suggests the development of rectilinear arrangements and simple, straight forms. The beam, however, may be curved in plan, tilted from the horizontal (as a roof rafter), or have other than a flat top or bottom. Posts can be T-shaped, Y-shaped, V-shaped, or multi-tiered. The system, in fact, lends itself to a greater degree of variation than practically any other system, which is one reason for its continuing widespread use (see Figure 5.13).

Materials can be separately considered for the post and beam. Masonry, for example, is a possibility for the post, but highly unlikely for the beam. In the main—for structures of building scale—the materials are limited to wood, stone and masonry, concrete, and steel. Let us consider a few possibilities and problems with these.

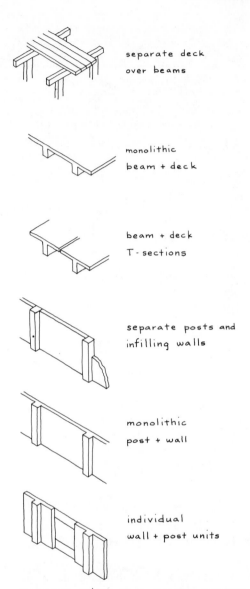

separate deck
over beams

monolithic
beam + deck

beam + deck
T-sections

separate posts and
infilling walls

monolithic
post + wall

individual
wall + post units

Figure 5.12 Infilling the post and beam system.

Wood Glue lamination and the use of complex built-up shapes can extend the form and scale possibilities of wood. Solid forms are limited to rectangular shapes. Fire resistance and dimensional instability are still problems. Recent innovations with composite wood–plywood systems open new system variations and form possibilities in wood.

Stone This was the material exploited by ancient cultures but is virtually unused in our time, except in masonry structures. The horizontal span of beams is highly restricted by the low tensile stress resistance in the material.

Masonry This has several advantages for posts, including fire resistance, stiffness, solidity, durability, and dimensional stability. A rather stout post, however, is inevitable. The connection between post and beam is limited in detail and types of feasible load transfer (see Figure 5.9).

Concrete Reinforced concrete overcomes the tensile limits of the basic stonelike material, making beams and rigid frame action of columns possible. Prestressing has extended the span limitations to a degree as yet unestablished.

More variation of form is possible in this material than in any other because of its cast production. Dimensional stability with time is generally good. However, the material has a time–strain characteristic—called the creep effect—that causes some sag accumulation with time in beams. Fire, rot, weathering, and wear resistance are all high.

Weight is generally a disadvantage, especially for beams. Compared to wood or steel, concrete is more than five times less efficient in strength-to-weight ratio. Weight reduction techniques (use of light-weight aggregate and hollow, or T-shapes) are of considerable significance for beams.

Steel The cost of this material dictates the use of hollow, I-shaped or T-shaped forms. Corrosion problems usually necessitate painting or other finishing. The need for fire resistance often requires that the steel be encased in insulative materials. The use of standard, factory-formed, linear elements is usually most practical. However, complex forms can be built up, at large or small scale, by welding or riveting.

Dimensional stability and other time

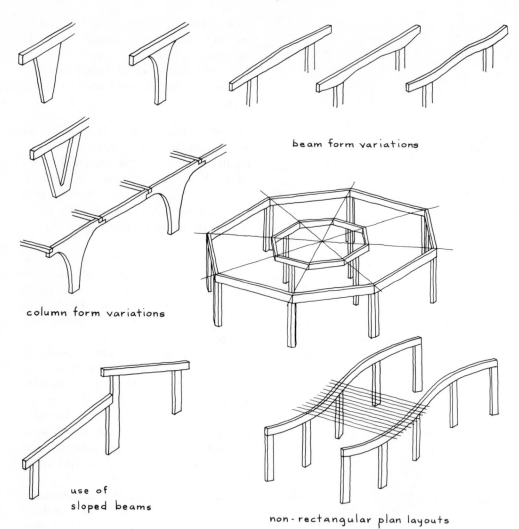

beam form variations

column form variations

use of
sloped beams

non-rectangular plan layouts

Figure 5.13 Form variations with the post and beam system.

factors are generally good. Rigid frames can be achieved easily by various connection techniques.

5.5 RIGID FRAME

When the members of a linear framework are rigidly attached—that is, when the joints are capable of transferring bending between the members—the system assumes a particular character. If all joints are rigid, it is impossible to load any one member transversely without causing bending in all members. This, plus the inherent stability of the system, are its unique aspects in comparison to the simple post and beam systems. The rigid frame action may be restricted to a single plane, or it may be extended in all directions in the three-dimensional framework (see Figure 5.14).

The joints take on a high degree of importance in this system. In fact, in the usual case, the highest magnitude of stresses and internal force are concentrated at the joints. If the frame is assembled from separate elements, the jointing must be studied carefully for structural function and feasibility.

A popular form of rigid frame is the gabled frame, in which two elements are

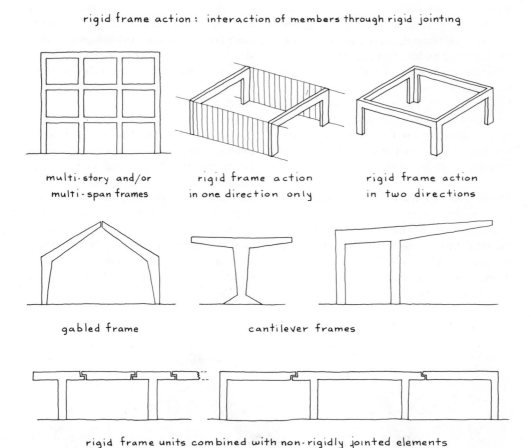

rigid frame action : interaction of members through rigid jointing

multi-story and/or
multi-span frames

rigid frame action
in one direction only

rigid frame action
in two directions

gabled frame

cantilever frames

rigid frame units combined with non-rigidly jointed elements

Figure 5.14 Rigid frames.

joined at the top of the gable peak, usually by a single hinge joint. This system is a logical one in laminated wood and is, in fact, one of the few possibilities for the rigid frame in wood. It is often used in steel or precast concrete as well.

Let us consider some of the problems and possibilities in the various materials.

Wood Jointing is difficult, two possibilities being the monolithic joint in laminated wood and the lapped joint. The laminated joint, or corner, is limited to angles larger than 90° and must usually be eased by

some radius of turn, rather than sharply made. The lapped joint is generally limited to small scale or to low magnitudes of moment transfer.

A recent innovation is the plywood-wood structure, in which webs or skins of plywood are used to provide continuity between the separate wood pieces.

Steel Welding can produce the highest degree of monolithicity in the steel frame, but bolting or riveting can also be used to produce rigid joints. These joints become very complex and must be carefully detailed. Frames are usually composed of stock linear elements (I, H, T, L, U, and tube), but may be produced in virtually any form by cutting and assembling steel plates and angles (see Figure 5.15).

A widely used system is the multi-storied, multibayed, steel cage frame for the high-rise building. Although the use of concrete is steadily climbing, the tallest buildings in the world to date use this framing system. The rigid framework alone is rather flexible in resisting horizontal forces, however, and is often braced by trussing or with infilling walls of reinforced concrete in order to increase its stiffness.

Reinforced Concrete The poured-in-place concrete framework is naturally rigid, since the joints are monolithic. Even when the structure is made by dividing the whole system into vertical and horizontal increments which are poured separately, this monolithic character is usually preserved—

for example, by keying or extending the reinforcing.

Precasting usually results in some loss of the monolithic character of the total system. This is not necessarily detrimental and may be reduced by casting units that are planar or even three-dimensional instead of all separate linear elements. Nevertheless, jointing of the elements is one of the most critical design problems in precast concrete frames.

Occasionally the rigid frame action is objectionable—for instance, when the beam transfers large bending to a small column or causes large curvature or kick at the base of a column. It is sometimes necessary to avoid the rigid frame action deliberately or to control it by using special joint detailing that controls the magnitude of bending or the actual joint turning, which can be transferred between the members.

Figure 5.15 Steel rigid frame. Welded steel elements produce a simple structure of clearly expressed function. Pump island canopy, Union Oil Company, Southern California.

Figure 5.16 shows four possibilities for the construction of a simple, single-span, rigid frame. While the basic profile form of the four alternatives may be the same, the construction details and the means for including joints for field erection is essentially unique for each of the basic materials used.

5.6 FLAT SPANNING SYSTEMS

Compared to the arch, the dome, or the draped catenary, the flat spanning structure is very hard-working. In fact, it is only exceeded by the cantilever in this respect. Consequently, scale limits can only be overcome by various techniques that im-

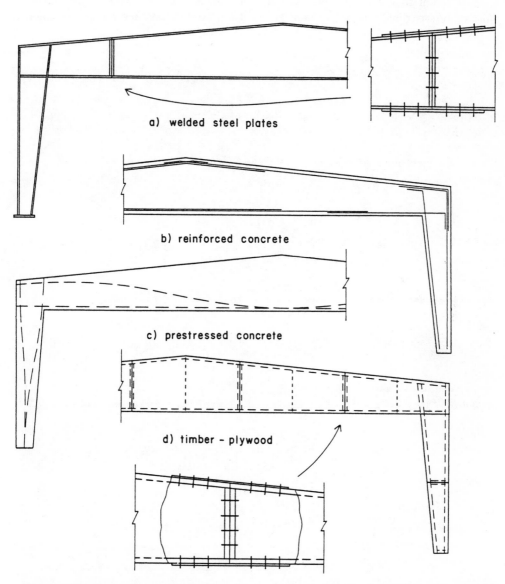

Figure 5.16 Four ways to construct a simple single span rigid frame. (From *Simplified Building Design for Wind and Earthquake Forces*, James Ambrose and Dimitry Vergun, John Wiley & Sons, New York, 1980, with permission.)

prove its efficiency. One of these is to develop the system as a two-way rather than a one-way spanning system. For a simple flat plate the load-bearing strength can thus be increased by almost 50 percent and the deflection reduced by an even higher degree (see Figure 5.17).

Maximum benefit is derived from two-way spanning if the spans are equal. The more different they become, the less the work in the long direction. At a ratio of 2 to 1, less than 10 percent of the resistance will be offered by the long span.

The other chief device for increasing efficiency is to improve the bending characteristic of the spanning elements. A simple example is the difference in effectiveness illustrated by a flat sheet of paper and one that has been pleated or corrugated. The real concept involved is that of increasing the depth of the element; the flat-sheet form has the least depth possible, whereas

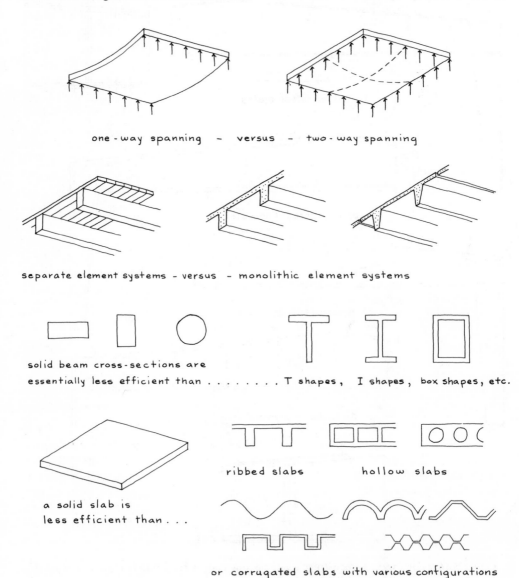

one-way spanning – versus – two-way spanning

separate element systems - versus - monolithic element systems

solid beam cross-sections are essentially less efficient than . . . . T shapes, I shapes, box shapes, etc.

a solid slab is less efficient than . . .

ribbed slabs   hollow slabs

or corrugated slabs with various configurations

Figure 5.17 Elements of flat spanning systems.

the sandwich panel with two sheets separated by considerable space is at the other extreme.

A critical relationship in the flat span, as in the beam, is the ratio of the span to the depth. Load capacity falls off rapidly as this ratio is pushed to its limits. Resistance to deflection is often more critical than resistance to the stresses in bending or shear.

Efficiency can also be increased by extending the element beyond its supports, by using monolithic elements continuous over several spans, or by developing bending transfer between the element and its supports (all the tricks already illustrated for the beam).

It is probably easiest to discuss specific systems for flat spanning in terms of materials.

Wood The simplest system is the flat wood deck made of wood boards or plywood. This is mostly used for short spans of a few feet or so. However, solid wood deck is available in up to 5.5 in. thickness for spans up to 20 ft. For longer spans, the system commonly used is that of a series of closely spaced wood beams, or joists, with a light wood deck spanning from joist to joist. As the span of the system increases, the spacing of the beams must be increased, so that for long spans there may be a second beam system of shorter span between the large beams.

Deflection is often the critical limitation for beam spans. The deck is limited by the need for eliminating bounciness, if it constitutes a floor. Sag with time is a critical problem in the flat-spanning wood structure.

Recent experimentation with plywood–wood elements have produced some new thinking for wood systems. Sandwich panels consisting of two faces of thin plywood separated by light wood joists are one possibility.

Steel Light sheet steel in corrugated or ribbed form is a widely used deck material

(see Figure 4.3). The deeper the ribs and the heavier the gage of the sheet, the longer the span possibilities. Units of this kind may be used for spans of up to 20 ft or more. However, the largest use is in the 5 to 10 ft range.

The corrugated surface is not useful for either flooring or roofing, and some filler element must be used. For roofs, the filler usually also functions as insulation. For floors, poured concrete is usually used for its stiffness, and its added weight gives solidity.

Beam and deck systems are useful in steel, and steel beams are used with a variety of other decks: wood, concrete, precast concrete, gypsum. A special system consists of steel beams tied to a concrete deck so that the two interact, the deck adding to the strength of the beams.

Light steel trusses—called open web joists, or bar joists—are widely used in place of steel beams. These are extremely efficient and are discussed under the subject of trusses.

A unique system is the two-way intersecting truss system for flat spans. This two-way continuity is possible because of the typical construction detailing of the steel truss system (Figures 5.22 and 5.23).

Reinforced Concrete Poured-in-place or precast concrete flat-span systems offer the largest variety of type and detail (Figure 5.18). Although wood and steel are largely limited to one-way spanning elements (except for the steel truss), concrete can achieve one-way or two-way spanning with equal dexterity.

One-Way Slab The simple solid slab is very useful, but limited to relatively short spans because of its weight and low efficiency. In special instances, weight reduction can be achieved by using forming elements to create hollow voids in the slab. Thus a slab several feet thick can be created.

One-Way Monolithic Beam and Slab This system is extensively used and is the

Figure 5.18 Concrete flat spanning systems. (*Upper left*) Traditional form of post and beam elements, executed in precast concrete. (*Upper right*) The ultimate flat-span use of the monolithic concrete in a two-way spanning slab without beams. Concentrated forces at the column are relieved by enlarging the top of the column. (*Lower left*) In the more efficient and sophisticated "waffle" system, the two-way spanning capability of the concrete is exploited by producing a grid of beams and a thin slab. The concentrated forces at the column are handled by making a heavy solid element around the column top. (*Lower right*) The two-way spanning potential of the poured concrete is developed in a large grid-beam roof. Great Western Savings and Loan Association, Gardena, California. Architects: Skidmore, Owings and Merrill, San Francisco.

most versatile system in terms of variations in layout, accommodation of special loads, and framed openings. The slab produces a T-beam action with the ribs, increasing their efficiency. A special case is the concrete joist system in which narrow beams are very closely spaced, emulating the traditional wood-joist construction. The slab thus becomes very thin—usually 2 to 3 in.—and the resulting structure is the lightest in weight of all flat-span concrete systems. Its relative lack of fire resistance, however, is a drawback.

Two-Way Slab, Edge Supported The spanning possibility of the solid slab is extended by capitalizing on the advantages already discussed. Edge supports may be monolithic beams or bearing walls.

Two-Way Slab, No Beams Called the flat slab, or flat plate system, this consists of only column supports and slab. The high concentration of stress in the slab in the vicinity of the column may be eased by widening the top of the column or by thickening the slab, or both.

Two-Way Ribbed Slab (Waffle) This is really a two-way grid of beams, possible only in monolithically cast concrete. Span limits are considerably longer than for the solid slab.

Corrugated or Folded Slab This is a giant version of the corrugated sheet steel deck. Span possibilities are considerable, especially with the use of prestressing. Intricate patterns of folding are possible.

Precast Units These may be simple solid or voided slab units, used in the same manner as the one-way solid slab, or units, for example, of T, U, F, and TT shape. The longest flat spans are currently achieved in concrete with these units, using prestressed reinforcing.

Prestressed Concrete Prestressing refers to a stress condition deliberately induced in an element before it sustains its loading stresses. The purpose is usually that of counteracting or canceling some of the stresses of the load. The most common means for imparting prestressing force to concrete is by stretching high-strength steel wire or cables (called tendons) inside the concrete mass in such a way that their tensile force is transferred to the concrete as compression, through bond or end anchoring of the tendons.

The two basic ways of prestressing with steel tendons are the following (see Figure 5.19).

Pretensioning The tendons are stretched inside the forms and the concrete is deposited around them. Once the concrete has hardened to a sufficient strength, the tendons are released and transmit the prestressing force by bonding to the concrete.

Posttensioning The tendons are inserted in holes in the precast concrete (or cast inside loose sleeves or conduits) and the tensile force is produced by anchoring the

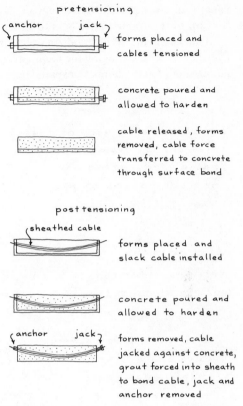

Figure 5.19 Prestressing concrete by pretensioning and posttensioning.

tendons at one end and stretching at the other end while pushing against the concrete. Once stretched, the tendons can be bonded to the concrete by pumping cement grout into the holes around the tendons. When the grout has hardened, the tendons can be released as in pretensioning.

5.7 TRUSS SYSTEMS

A framework of linear elements connected by joints can be stabilized independently by guys, struts, or rigid infilling panels. If it is internally stabilizing, or self-stabilizing, it becomes so through one of two means. The first is the use of rigid joints, as previously discussed. This results both in shear and bending in the members of the frame and usually in considerable movement or deflection of the frame under lateral loads.

The second means of stabilizing a linear framework is by arranging the members in patterns of planar triangles or spatial tetrahedrons (see Figure 5.20). This is called

trussing, and when the structural element produced is a flat-spanning or cantilevering planar unit, it is called simply a truss. The triangulated frame can also be used to produce other structural forms such as rigid frames, arches, three-dimensional

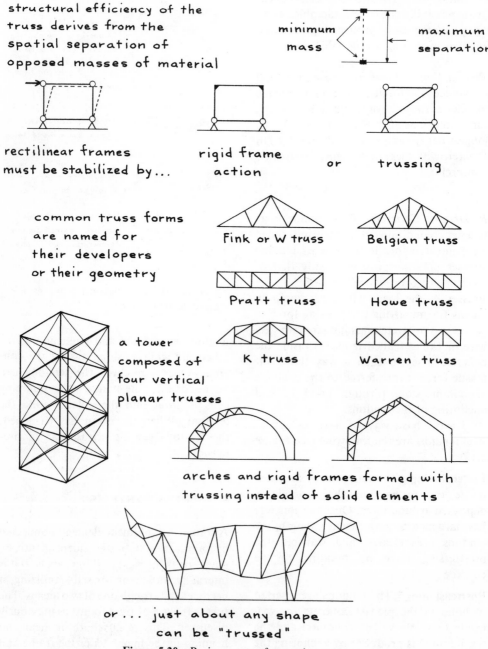

Figure 5.20 Basic aspects of trussed structures.

towers, and two-way flat span systems. If the overall element has some other classification, it is referred to as a trussed arch or a trussed tower.

The triangular subdivision of the planar system, or the tetrahedral subdivision of the spatial system, produces geometric units that are nondeformable—that is, the arrangement cannot be changed without changing the length of a member or disconnecting a joint. This is one of the basic concepts at work in the truss. The other is the technique of causing widely spaced small masses of material to interact, giving the ultimate maximum efficiency in bending resistance (see the discussion of bending efficiency in Chapter 3).

The multiplicity of joints in the trussed system makes their detailing a major item in truss design. The logic of form of the linear members derives as much, if not more, from the jointing as from their function as tension-resistive or compression-resistive elements. The elimination of bending and shear in the members is, by the way, another basic concept of the truss and is actually or essentially achieved in many trusses. The less flexible the joints and the stouter the members, the less the "pure" truss action.

An almost infinite variety of truss configurations is possible. The particular configuration, the loads sustained, the scale, the material, and the jointing methods are all design considerations. Let us consider some of the materials and possibilities.

Wood Wood trusses of considerable size were used hundreds of years ago, long before any rational analysis procedures were developed. Today we use wood trusses mostly for short to medium spans (20 to 100 ft). Modern jointing techniques, the use of steel tension members, and the emphasis on factory prefabrication, make contemporary wood trusses considerably different from their ancient predecessors (see Figure 5.21).

A very widely used wood truss is the small W-shaped truss of light two-by-fours or two-by-sixes, used to form the gable roof of wood-framed residences. Another popular form is the bowstring truss, actually in the form of a tied arch.

A great advantage of the truss is the low

Figure 5.21 Large 120 ft span wood bowstring trusses form the roof of this factory in Minnesota.

deflection that results under load, if adequate depth-to-span ratios are maintained.
The W-shaped truss of light wood experi-
ences virtually no deflection under a working load, as compared to a flat span beam
system of heavy timbers for the same span.

A currently popular jointing system for
the light wood truss uses plywood joint
panels, called "gussetts," which are glued to
all members at a joint. The truss is thus
actually glued together. Larger-scale
trusses usually consist of multiple-piece
members that intertwine at the joints, like
your fingers when your hands meet in the
praying gesture. Special metal locking devices, called shear developers are sometimes used between the faces of the overlapping wood pieces; the joint is then tied
by bolting.

Steel Steel trusses are used at both
extremes of scale. The small truss previously referred to as the open-web joist
(Figure 4.3), is widely used for building
roofs and floors of short to medium span.
These are factory assembled and installed
like wood or steel beams. At the other end
of the scale is the great steel cantilever truss
of the Quebec Bridge, built in 1917, which

leaps over the St. Lawrence River with a
clear center span of 1800 ft.

One of the great engineering tours de
force of all time, the Eiffel Tower, is a
trussed steel structure. The tallest human
made structure in the world is a trussed
steel shaft television transmission tower,
guyed by steel cables.

Steel offers a much wider range of
jointing and member forms than wood
does. In the small open-web joist the
members may be simple solid rods, light T's
or L's, or even heavy gage sheet metal
folded to form shapes. Jointing at small
scale is usually by simple direct welding of
members to each other. As the scale increases, the form of the members and the
jointing become more complex. The largest
members in the Quebec Bridge and the
Eiffel Tower are themselves huge structural
elements several feet in diameter.

The two-way truss—often called a
space frame, although the term is confusing
—has been developed largely in steel (Figure 5.22). A small-scale system developed
by the Unistrut Corporation consists of
what are actually small-dimension scaffolding elements, assembled by simple
bolting in patterns that generate from a

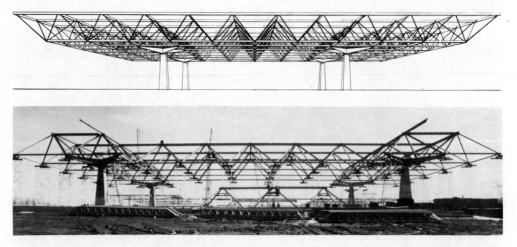

Figure 5.22 Two-way spanning steel truss supported on only four columns. The columns have
four-fingered tops to reduce the concentrated effects of force in the truss. Overall size of the roof
is 216 by 297 ft. Pekin High School Gym, Pekin, Illinois. Architects: Foley, Hackler, Thompson
and Lee, Peoria, Illinois. Structural engineers: The Engineers Collaborative, Chicago.

basic modular unit in the form of a square-based pyramid.

A large-scale two-way truss was used for the roof of the main dining hall in the Air Force Academy at Colorado Springs, Colorado. The truss is square, with clear span of 266 ft and projected edges of 21 ft. The pattern is simply that of intersecting vertical plane trusses (see Figure 5.23).

Reinforced Concrete Inconceivable as it seems, there has been considerable exploitation of the reinforced concrete truss. The advent of higher quality materials, fine production workmanship through factory casting, and prestressed reinforcing techniques have made this increasingly feasible. A major advantage is that jointing is virtually eliminated since members are cast

Figure 5.23 This large, square roof has intersecting, vertical-planar steel trusses supported on four sides by columns. The roof spans 266 ft and cantilevers 21 ft at the sides. Assembly of the trusses was performed at ground level and the entire roof structure was lifted into position by jacks positioned on the tops of the columns. Air Force Academy dining hall, Colorado Springs, Colorado. Architects and engineers: Skidmore, Owings,.and Merrill, Chicago.

monolithically as one. Resistance to fire
and deterioration are other possible attributes. Weight is obviously a disadvantage,
but not really unsurmountable, since the
system itself has such a high degree of
efficiency. Two-way spanning and other
spatial truss systems of precast concrete
units offer interesting and promising possibilities for development.

5.8   ARCH, VAULT, AND DOME SYSTEMS

The basic concept in the arch is the development of a spanning structure through
the use of only internal compression (see
Figure 5.24). The profile of the "pure" arch
may actually be geometrically derived from
the loading and support conditions. For a

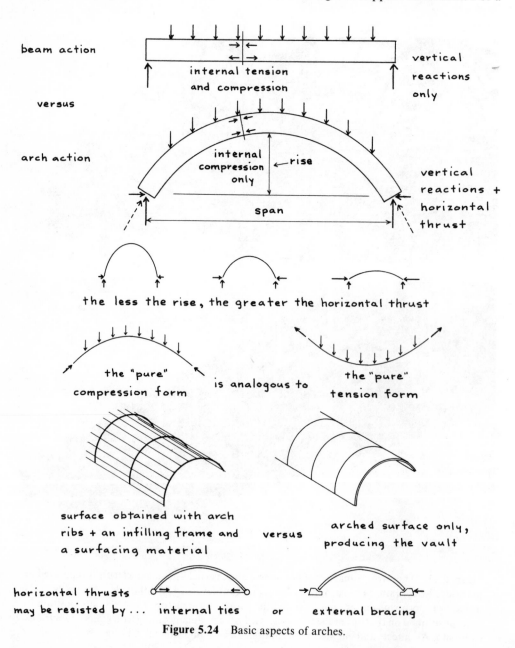

Figure 5.24   Basic aspects of arches.

single-span arch with no fixity at the base in the form of moment resistance, with supports at the same level, and with a uniformly distributed load on the entire span, the resulting form is that of a second-degree curve, or a parabola. Various other curves—circular or elliptical—can be used, but the basic form is that of the familiar curve, convex downward, if the load is primarily gravity.

Basic considerations are the necessary horizontal forces at the base from thrust and the ratio of span to rise. As this ratio increases, the thrust increases, producing higher compression in the arch and larger horizontal forces at the support.

In the great stone arches of old the principal load was gravity—the weight of the arch itself. Although other forces existed, they were usually incidental in magnitude compared to the gravity force. In contemporary construction, the lightness of the structure has changed this situation, virtually eliminating the possibility of the pure arch. Horizontal forces of wind or seismic movement, or even uplift from aerodynamic effects, require the consideration of more than simple gravity force in deriving the arch form and detail. Consequently, most arches today are continuous ribs of steel, laminated wood, reinforced concrete, or trussed configurations—all capable of considerable bending and shear—in addition to the basic arch compression.

The thrust of the arch—that is, the horizontal component of it—is resolved in one of two ways. The most direct way is to balance the force at one support against that at the other simply by using a tension tie across the base of the arch. This very possibly, however, destroys the internal space defined by the arch and is therefore not always acceptable. The second way is to resolve each kick separately, outside the arch. This means creating a heavy abutment, or, if the arch rests on the top of a wall or a column, creating a strut or a buttress for the wall or column.

If adjacent arches are assembled side-by-side in a row perpendicular to their planes, the vault is produced—that is, a surface, rather than a planar rib, is obtained. If vaults intersect, complex three-dimensional forms are created in the lines of intersection. The forms resulting from intersecting vaults and the ribs placed at the intersection lines and edges were the main structural essence of the Gothic church construction.

If the single arch is rotated in place about its crown, or apex, the form generated is a dome. This structural form relates to a circle in plan, in contrast to the vault, which relates to a rectangle, or cross form.

Both vault and dome forms can be created as ribbed (that is, a set of skeleton arches with an infilling shell) or as direct shell forms. In our time few arches, vaults, or domes are made of cut stone. Reinforced concrete is probably the most obvious material for the shell forms, although ribbed systems are equally feasible in laminated wood or steel. Vaults of plywood are currently used extensively, and "bubble" dome forms in plastic are the most widely used skylight elements. Let us briefly consider the materials for these structures.

Wood Laminated wood ribs have been used for arch and dome structures of large scale. At smaller scale the plywood vault—of single-sheet thickness or in sandwich form—is an alternative. The availability of larger sheets than the traditional 4-by-8 ft size has increased the possibilities of this system. The shell of plywood sheets or wood planks or boards can be used over steel ribs as well as over wood ones.

Steel The steel arch, in solid or trussed form, has been used for very great spans. It is also feasible for small structures. Ribs are often produced by simple cold bending of straight steel elements for short spans. Vault surfaces can be produced with sheet steel in corrugated form. Domes can be produced from formed plates, welded, or riveted, for instance, as for large tanks. At very small scale, sheet steel can be deformed by stamping to form domical shapes, for instance, car bodies.

Reinforced Concrete   Precast concrete is an alternative for the single arch rib. Poured-in-place concrete can be used for either shell vaults and domes or for monolithic rib and shell systems. These systems seem natural for concrete, especially since its greatest attribute is its compressive resistance.

Masonry and Stone   These materials have been largely replaced by others in today's construction of arches, vaults, and domes. What may appear to be a cut stone or masonry dome today is most likely simply a structure with an applied finish of cut stone, or even simulated stone molded in plaster. The actual supporting structure may not even be an arch or dome at all, but a steel truss. It is merely a matter of economics and available skilled workers.

Plastic   There are great possibilities for vault and dome systems in plastic. In sandwich form or composite plastic–metal or concrete ribs, small- to medium-span roof structures are perfectly feasible. The simple one-piece plastic bubble has already been extended to more than 12 ft in span (see Figure 4.10).

5.9   TENSION STRUCTURES

The tension suspension structure was highly developed by some primitive societies through the use of vines or strands woven from grass or shredded bamboo. These structures achieved impressive spans; foot bridges spanning 100 ft have been recorded. The development of steel, however, heralded the great span capability of this system. At first in chain and link, and later in the cable woven of drawn wire, the

suspension structure quickly took over as the long-span champion (see Figure 5.25).

Structurally, the single draped cable is merely the inverse of the arch in both geometry and internal force (see Figure 5.26). The compression-arch parabola is merely flipped over to produce the tension cable. Span-to-sag ratio and horizontal inward thrust at the supports have their parallels in the arch behavior.

Additional problems with the suspension element are its lack of stiffness, which causes reforming under load changes and possible fluttering or flapping, and the more difficult connection at its supports. The latter is due to basic differences between transfer of compression and tension.

Steel is obviously the principal material for this system, and the cable is the logical form. Actually the largest spans use clusters of cables—up to 3 ft in diameter for the Golden Gate Bridge with its 4000 ft span. While a virtually solid steel element 3 ft in diameter hardly seems flexible, one must consider the span-to-thickness ratio— approximately 1330 to 1. This is like a 1 in. diameter rod over 100 ft long. One cannot anchor this size element by tying a clove hitch around a stake!

Structures can also be hung simply by tension elements. The deck of the suspension bridge, for instance, is not placed directly on the cables but is hung with another system of cables. Cantilevers or spanning systems may thus be supported by hanging as well as by columns, piers, or walls.

There are many possibilities for the utilization of tension elements in structures in addition to the simple draped or vertically hung cable. Cables can be arranged in a circular, radiating pattern with an inner tension hub and an outer compression rim similar to those in a bicycle wheel (see Figure 5.27). Cables can also be arranged in criss-crossing networks, as draped systems, or as restraining elements for air-inflated membrane surfaces.

Tension surface structures can be pro-

Figure 5.25 Oakland Bay Bridge, San Francisco, California. Trussed steel towers support the long-span, draped steel cables. Vertical hanger cables attached to the spanning cables support the steel trussed roadway structure.

duced by direct tensioning, for instance, in the familiar fabric tent. A more recent innovation is that of the tension membrane surface maintained by air inflation.

5.10 SURFACE STRUCTURES

The neatness of our categorization of structural systems eventually breaks down, since variations within one system tend to produce different systems, and overlapping between categories exists. Thus the rigidly connected post and beam become the rigid frame. Surface structures are essentially those consisting of relatively thin, extensive surfaces functioning primarily by resolving only internal forces within their surfaces (see Figure 5.28).

Figure 5.29 shows the difference between in-plane and out-of-plane force resolution. We have already discussed several surface structures. The wall in resisting compression, in stabilizing the building by resisting in-plane shear, and in spanning like a beam acts as a surface structure. The vault and the dome are really surface structures. These can also develop nonsurface actions, however. The wall, in bending under loads perpendicular to its surface, develops out-of-plane action.

The purest surface structures are ten-

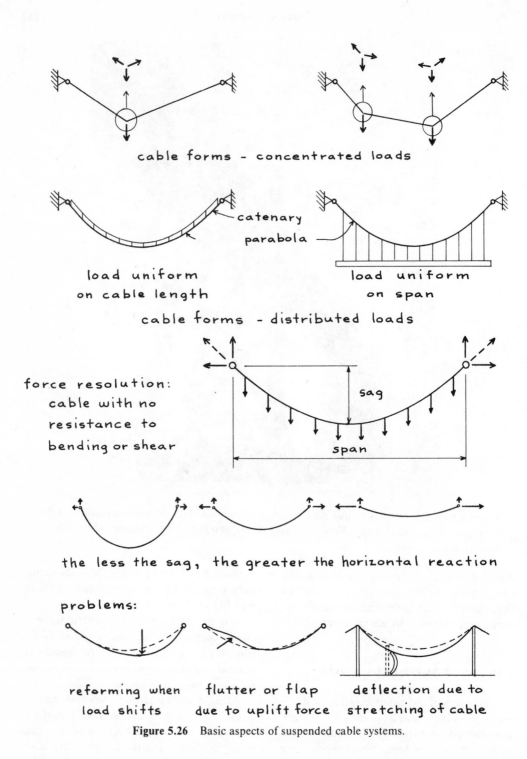

cable forms - concentrated loads

catenary
parabola

load uniform
on cable length

load uniform
on span

cable forms - distributed loads

force resolution:
cable with no
resistance to
bending or shear

sag

span

the less the sag, the greater the horizontal reaction

problems:

reforming when
load shifts

flutter or flap
due to uplift force

deflection due to
stretching of cable

Figure 5.26 Basic aspects of suspended cable systems.

sion surfaces, since they are often made of materials incapable of any significant out-of-plane resistance. Thus the canvas tent, the rubber balloon, and the plastic bag are all limited in capability to tension resistance within the planes of their surfaces. The forms they assume, then, must all be completely "pure." In fact, the pure compression surface is sometimes derived by simulating it in reverse with a tension surface (see Figures 4.11 and 5.30).

Compression surfaces must be more rigid than tension ones, because of the possibility of buckling. This increased stiffness makes them difficult to use in a way that avoids developing out-of-plane bending and shear.

Compression resistive surface structures of curved form are also called shells. The egg, the light bulb, the plastic bubble, and the auto fender are all examples of shells. At the building scale the most extensively exploited material for this system has been reinforced concrete (Figures 2.2, 5.31, and 5.32). The largest structure of this type is that of an exposition hall in France with clear span of 700 ft. The structure is a concrete shell of double, or sandwich, form.

Both simple and complex geometries

Figure 5.27 Tension structure. New York State's "Tent of Tomorrow" pavilion at the 1964–1965 World's Fair. The 100-ft-high, slip-formed concrete columns carry a steel compression ring that is 350 ft by 250 ft and elliptical in plan. Suspended from the ring, a double layer of prestressed steel cables converge toward a steel tension ring at the center. The roof surface consists of translucent sandwich panels formed of two sheets of fiberglass-reinforced plastic, separated by an aluminum grid. The panels, approximately 3000 in number, are trapezoidal in plan and vary from 3 to 17 ft in length and 3 to 4 ft in width. Architect: Phillip Johnson Associates, New York. Structural Engineer: Lev Zetlin and Associates, New York. Plastic panels: Filon Corporation. Photo: Filon Corporation.

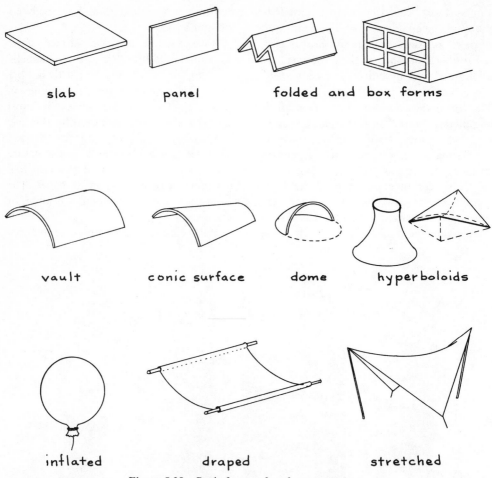

slab   panel   folded and box forms

vault   conic surface   dome   hyperboloids

inflated   draped   stretched

Figure 5.28   Basic forms of surface structures.

are possible with shells. Edges, corners, openings, and point supports are potential locations of high stress and out-of-plane bending; consequently reinforcing is often necessary, usually consisting of monolithically cast ribs in concrete. The existence of these stiffening ribs often alters the pure surface structure character of the shells and results in complex behaviors, for example, with aspects of arch or rigid-frame action.

A special variation of the shell is the surface produced by multiple folds or pleats. The overall form of the structure may assume curvature, but the individual elements are all flat surfaces. These structures are referred to as folded plates. They

lend themselves to execution in plywood or sheet metal as well as concrete. There is some advantage in the ease of forming the flat surfaces and the straight-line intersections (see Figure 4.2).

5.11   SPECIAL SYSTEMS

Most of the common systems have now been itemized. Innumerable special systems are possible, each creating a new category by its unique aspects. Briefly described, some of these follow:

Inflated Structures   Inflation, or air pressure, can be used as a structural device in a

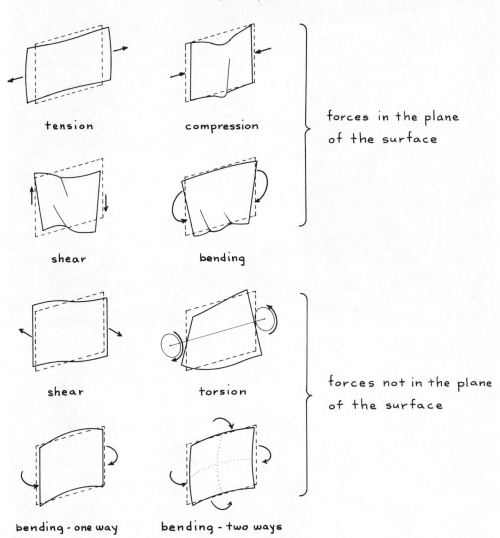

tension

compression

forces in the plane
of the surface

shear

bending

shear

torsion

forces not in the plane
of the surface

bending - one way

bending - two ways

Figure 5.29 Force resolution in surface structures.

variety of ways (see Figure 5.33). Simple internal inflation of a totally enclosing membrane surface, for instance, in the simple rubber balloon (Figure 4.11) is the most direct. This requires about the least structural material imaginable for spanning. The structure is unavoidably highly flexible, however, and dependent on the constant differential between inside and outside pressure. It is also necessarily "lumpy" in form, because the surface is stretched. It has nevertheless been utilized for buildings of considerable size.

A second use of inflation is the stiffening of a structural element. This can be a sandwich or hollow ribbed structure of tension membrane material given a rigid frame character by inflation of the voids within the structural element, for example, the inflated inner tube or air mattress. The need for sealing the space enclosed by the structure is thus eliminated (see Figure 5.30).

A third possibility is that of using a combination of inflation and simple tension draping or stretching on a frame. Thus

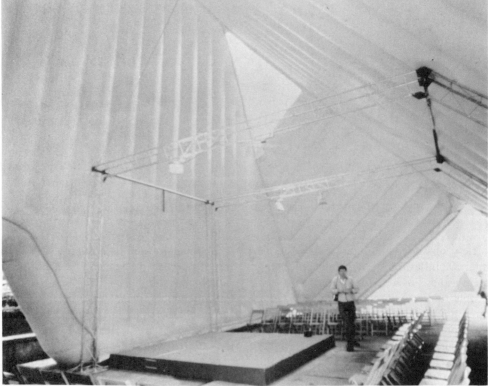

Figure 5.30 Air-inflated structure for the Three-Rivers Arts Festival, Pittsburgh, Pennsylvania, 1976. Double surfaced elements, analogous to air mattresses, form this pavillion structure. Designers and builders: Chrysalis East, Milwaukee, Wisconsin. Photos: Joseph Valerio.

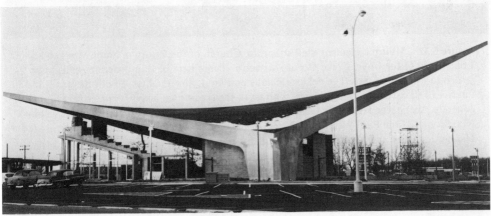

Figure 5.31 Concrete hyperbolic-paraboloid shell. Supported at only two points, the 4 in. thick shell spans 159 ft between abutments and measures 221 ft from tip to tip of the cantilevered ends. Concrete for the abutments, edge beams, and shell was poured in a single, continuous operation. Edens Theater, Northbrook, Illinois. Architects: Perkins and Will, Chicago. Structural engineers: The Engineers Collaborative, Chicago. Photo: Gibson Studios, Chicago.

the pillow can be suspended—its lower surface draped in tension and its upper surface maintained by inflation. An advantage in this system is the elimination of the water pocket normally formed by the draping of a surface.

Lamella Frameworks This is a system for forming arch or dome surfaces utilizing a network of perpendicular ribs that appear to be diagonal in plan. It has been used at both modest and great spans and has been executed in wood, steel, and precast concrete. One great advantage is in the repetition of similar size elements and joint details. Another advantage is in the use of straight-line elements to produce the curved vault surface (see Figure 5.34).

Geodesic Domes A few lines can scarcely do justice to this system. Developed from ideas innovated by R. Buckminster Fuller,

Figure 5.32   Multiple-element shell structure. Church of the Priory of Saint Mary and Saint Louis, School for Boys, Creve Coeur, Missouri. Three tiers of thin concrete shells form the structure for this chapel. The delicate details and light, airy quality of both the exterior and interior of this structure are in sharp contrast to the traditional heavy, crude aspect of poured concrete. Architects: Hellmuth, Obata and Kassabaum, St. Louis. Structural engineers: John P. Nix, St. Louis, and Paul Weidlinger, New York City. Photo: James K. Mellow, St. Louis, from Hellmuth, Obata and Kassabaum.

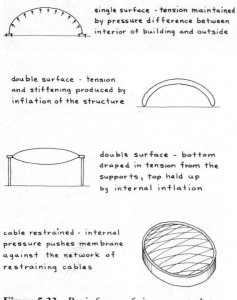

single surface - tension maintained by pressure difference between interior of building and outside

double surface - tension and stiffening produced by inflation of the structure

double surface - bottom draped in tension from the supports, top held up by internal inflation

cable restrained - internal pressure pushes membrane against the network of restraining cables

Figure 5.33   Basic forms of air-supported structures.

this technique for forming hemispherical surfaces is based on spherical triangulation (see Figure 5.35). It is also useful at both small and large scales and subject to endless variation of detail, member configuration, and materials. In addition to ordinary wood, steel, and concrete, it has been executed in plywood, plastic, cardboard, bamboo, and aluminum (see Figure 4.8).

The chief attributes of the system are its multiplication of basic units and joints and the extreme efficiency of its internal force resolution. Its developers claim that its efficiency increases with size, making it difficult to see any basis for establishing a limiting scale.

Mast Structures   These are structures similar to trees, having single legs for vertical support and supporting one or a

Figure 5.34 Wood lamella structure. Simple wood elements in lamella pattern form this 109 ft span roof for a bowling alley in Detroit, Michigan. Architects: Hawthorne and Schmiedeke, Detroit. Photo: American Institute of Timber Construction, Washington, D. C.

Figure 5.35 Geodesic dome structure. Climatron, Missouri Botanical Gardens, St. Louis, Missouri. This 175 ft diameter dome has plastic glazing of Plexiglas suspended from its geodesic frame of tubular aluminum elements. Architects: Murphy and Mackey, St. Louis. Photo: Rohm and Haas Company, Philadelphia.

Figure 5.35 (continued)

112

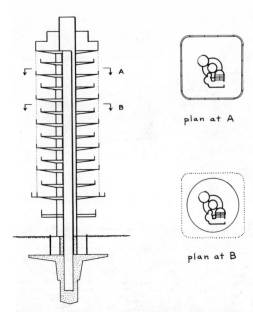

plan at A

plan at B

Figure 5.36 Tower structure—mast form. Laboratory Tower, Johnson Wax Company, Racine, Wisconsin. A central core supports alternating square and round floors in this treelike structure. The taproot foundation firmly plants the structure in the ground. Architect: Frank Lloyd Wright.

series of "branches". They obviously require very stable bases, well anchored against the overturning effect of horizontal forces. Their chief advantage lies in the minimum of space occupied by the base (see Figure 5.36).

Multiple   Monopode   Units Multiple mushroom, lily-pad, or morning-glory form elements can be used to produce the one-story building of many horizontal increments. Principally developed with reinforced concrete shell forms, this system offers savings in the repetitive use of a single form (see Figure 5.37). An exciting example in steel at large scale is the exhibition building in Turin, Italy by Pier Luigi Nervi.

This brief sampling does not pretend to present the complete repertoire of contemporary structural systems for buildings. The continual development of new materials, systems, and construction processes keeps this a dynamic area of endeavor. New systems are added; established ones outmoded. Modern techniques of analysis and design make the rational, reliable design of complex systems feasible.

One seemingly inevitable trend is that toward the industrialization of the building process. This tends to emphasize those materials, systems, and processes that lend themselves to industrial production. Prefabrication, modular coordination, component systems, and machine-produced details are increasingly evident in our building structures. Although the handcrafted structure will always have a certain charm, the increasing use of industrialized

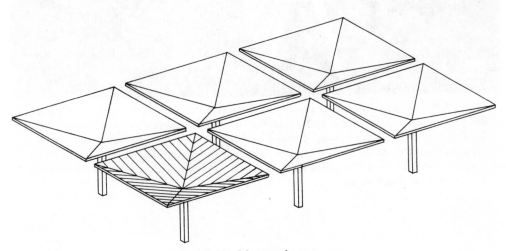

Figure 5.37 Monopode structure.

Figure 5.38 Industrially produced building system. This large-scale steel space structure was designed for the U.S. Air Force by Konrad Wachsmann under a research grant during 1959–1961. Use of only two dimensions of round steel tube and a single common joint capable of accommodating up to 20 members at one node, simplifies erection and allows for ultimate realization of mass-production advantages. The structure is completely demountable for reuse. Photos: Konrad Wachsmann.

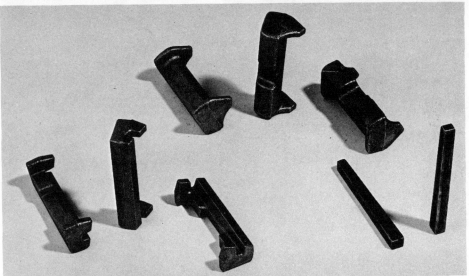

Figure 5.39 Assembled joint and its elements for Wachsmann's hangar structure.

products and systems will undoubtedly continue. A study of the work of pioneers in the use of industrial products for building structures, such as Joseph Paxton, Gustave Eiffel, Henri Labrouste, James Bogardus, Alexander Graham Bell, Walter Gropius, and Konrad Wachsmann (see Figure 5.38 and 5.39), reveals the prophetic nature of their ideas reflected in the evolving technology of our present time.

As the complexity, sophistication, and sheer diversity of our structural vocabulary

expands without visible limits, the problem
of selecting the proper solution for each
case becomes more difficult. It is clearly
beyond the capacity of an individual to
know the potentialities and limitations of
all conceivable alternatives for each problem. Although personal experience and
first-hand knowledge can never be replaced, it is hoped that intelligent use of
modern data-processing facilities will make
useful information more readily available
to the designer, thus making optimal design
a possibility for all designers who avail
themselves of the facility.

CHAPTER SIX

From the Ground Up

Most buildings rest on the ground. Thus all of the loads on the building must eventually be transferred to the ground. The interfacing element between the building and the ground that conducts this transfer is the building foundation.

6.1 THE GROUND

So-called solid ground is usually made up of soil or rock. Soil is ground material consisting of discrete particles that can be separated relatively easily by water or by some mechanical means such as digging, squeezing, or scratching. Rock is material that is excessively hard to excavate and is generally not affected by water.

All soils have some degree of compressibility, so the transfer of load to them produces some movement. Because of this, vertical gravity loads from a building usually cause some vertical downward movement of the foundations, called settlement.

For most building designs, an investigation of the ground conditions is made in order to establish the capability of the soil to sustain the anticipated loads. The two primary concerns are for the total soil strength and its relative compressibility. For both design and construction purposes, however, it is also usually useful to know other properties of the soil as well as the amount of water in the soil mass.

6.2 FOUNDATION SYSTEMS

Once the ground conditions are known and some preliminary information is established regarding the proposed construction, consideration can be given to the choice of the foundation system. The two basic types of foundations are shallow bearing systems and deep systems.

Shallow bearing foundations consist of elements that bear directly on the ground immediately beneath the building. The primary elements of such a system are footings, commonly consisting of simple pads and strips of concrete formed by pouring the concrete directly into a shallow excavation. The footings are usually combined with foundation walls and various other elements to form the whole building foundation system. Figure 6.1 shows some of the elements that ordinarily constitute the foundation system for a building with shallow bearing footings.

Occasionally it is not possible to use shallow bearing footings because the soil immediately below the building is too weak or too compressible, or because of potential problems of erosion, subsidence, and other unstabilizing effects on the upper soil mass. When these situations occur it is usually necessary to utilize some type of deep foundation. The types most commonly used are piles and piers, shown in Figure 6.2.

Piles consist of linear elements that are driven into the ground like large nails. They

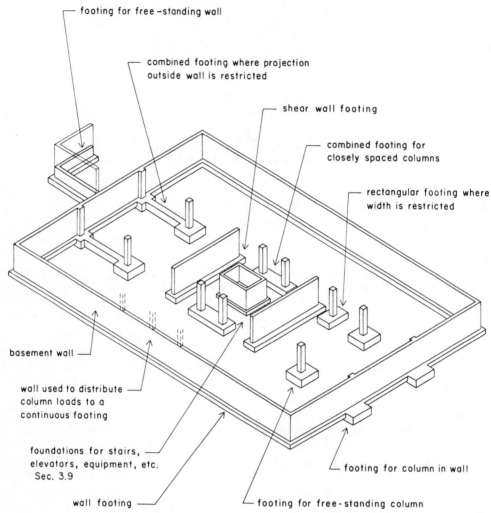

— footing for free-standing wall

— combined footing where projection
outside wall is restricted

— shear wall footing

— combined footing for
closely spaced columns

— rectangular footing where
width is restricted

basement wall —

wall used to distribute —
column loads to a
continuous footing

foundations for stairs, —
elevators, equipment, etc.
Sec. 3.9

wall footing —

— footing for free-standing column

— footing for column in wall

Figure 6.1   Typical elements of bearing foundation systems.

can be made of wood, steel, or concrete, and can be driven until their ends bear on rock (called end-bearing piles) or simply until their embedded lengths develop the

necessary load resistance (called friction piles).

The pile driving process permits only a limited control of the location at the top of the driven pile. For this reason, as well as to accumulate more total load-carrying capacity, piles are usually driven in groups, called clusters. A single pile cluster is usually joined together by a poured concrete cap. The complete building foundation can resemble one with shallow bearing footings—pile caps simply replace the footings.

Piers are also vertical shafts formed by excavating the shaft form in the soil and

piles – dynamically driven   piers – excavated

end-bearing   friction   end-bearing,   belled bottom
                              shaft only

Figure 6.2   Basic types of deep foundations.

then filling the excavation with concrete. Piers function essentially the same as end-bearing piles and are typically excavated to bear on rock or a very dense soil layer. When bearing on rock, the shaft is usually a constant cylindrical form. When bearing on soil, the lower end is usually flared out to produce a conical, bell-shaped form that increases the surface for bearing.

When piers are excavated below the ground water level, they are sometimes built by the caisson method used for the construction of bridge piers. It is still common practice to refer to piers as caissons, even though this excavation method is not used.

When a shallow bearing foundation can be used, its selection is usually obvious, since the cost of deep foundations is typically much greater.

6.3 ABOVE-GROUND SUPPORTS

Foundations are often essentially out of view, and the building is fit snugly to the ground with only a thin top edge of the foundation visible. There are some situations, however, in which the building is held above the ground. One way to achieve this is simply to extend the foundation above the ground level (Figure 6.3).

In some cases the building is supported on legs, piers, pylons, and so on. These may be merged with elements of the foundation system or may constitute a third system transitional between the foundation and the building structure. An example of this is shown in Figure 6.4. This technique may be used essentially as an architectural design device—the building conceived as a layered structure with one element stacked

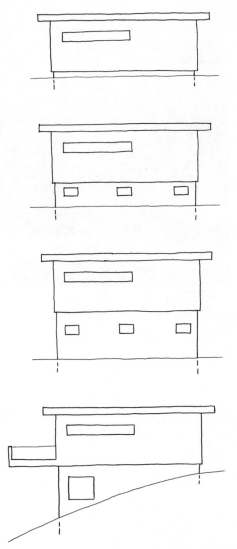

Figure 6.3 Building base formed by upward extension of the foundation structure.

on top of the other. However, it is also used when there is some functional reason to keep the building above the ground, for instance, the need for open space below the building for pedestrians or vehicles.

Figure 6.4 Transitional support elements used to raise the building free of the ground. CN Park Place office building, Los Angeles. Architects: Langdon and Wilson, Los Angeles.

Glossary

The following definitions of words and terms are given to assist the reader. As much as possible, the definitions are those that are established, or in common usage, in the professions.

Acceleration In engineering mathematics: the rate of change of the velocity of a moving object, or $a = dv/dt$. Indicates that the state of motion is changing from motion to rest, from rest to motion, from one speed to another. Occurs when the forces acting on an object are unbalanced. Negative acceleration is called deceleration. *See* Motion.

Adequate Just enough; sufficient. Indicates a quality of bracketed acceptability—on the one hand not insufficient, on the other, not superlative or excessive.

Aggregate In concrete terminology, the loose, inert material that makes up the major portion of the bulk of the concrete. It is bound into a monolithic mass by water and cement mortar.

Amplitude *See* Vibration.

Analysis Separation into constituent parts. In engineering, the investigative determination of the detail aspects of a particular phenomenon. May be qualitative, meaning a general evaluation of the nature of the phenomenon, or quantitative, meaning the numerical determination of the magnitude of the phenomenon. *See* Synthesis.

Anchorage Attachment for resistance to movement, usually to that induced by uplift, overturn, sliding or horizontal separation.

Assemblage Something put together from parts. A random, unordered assemblage is called a gathering. An ordered assemblage is a system.

Beam A structural element that sustains transverse loading and develops internal forces of bending and shear in resisting the loads. Also called a girder if large-scale; a joist if small-scale or used in a closely spaced series; a rafter if used for a roof.

Bending Turning action that causes change in the curvature of a linear element. Characterized by the development of opposed internal stresses of tension and compression. *See* Moment.

Box system A structural system in which lateral loads are not resisted by a frame with rigid joints but rather by shear walls or a braced (trussed) frame.

Buckling Collapse, in the form of sudden sideways deflection, of a slender element subjected to compression.

Caisson *See* Pier.

Calculation Ordered, rational determination, usually by mathematical methods.

Component Part of a system. May designate one of the distinct pieces of an assembled mechanism or one aspect of an action (such as the uplift effect of wind).

Compression   Force that tends to crust adjacent particles of a material together and cause overall shortening in the direction of its action.

Connection   The union or joining of two or more distinct elements. In a structure, the connection itself often becomes an entity. Thus the actions of the parts on each other may be visualized in terms of their action on the connection.

Continuity   Used to describe structures or parts of structures whose behavior is influenced by the monolithic, continuous nature of adjacent elements, such as continuous vertical multistory columns, continuous multispan beams, and rigid frames.

Crawl space   Space between the underside of the floor construction and the ground surface that exists when a framed floor is suspended above ground and there is no basement.

Creep   Plastic deformation that proceeds with time when certain materials, such as concrete and lead, are subjected to constant, long-duration stress.

Damping   *See* Vibration.

Dead Load   *See* Load.

Deflection   The movement of the surface, profile, or position of a structure away from an original shape, as the sag of a loaded beam. *Deflected shape* refers to the overall distorted form of the loaded structure.

Density   *See* Mass.

Design   The conception, contrivance, or planning of a work (verb). The descriptive image of the proposed work (noun). *See* Synthesis.

Determinate   Having defined limits; definite. In structures, the condition of having exact sufficiency of stability externally and internally, therefore being determinable by the resolution of force alone. An excess of

stability conditions produces a structure characterized as indeterminate or indeterminable.

Diaphragm   A solid surface element (plywood deck, masonry wall, etc.) used to resist forces in its own plane by spanning or by cantilevering. *See* Shear Wall.

Ductility   The ability to deform considerably under load before fracturing. Contrasted to the quality of brittleness.

Dynamic   Implies motion or change of state; opposite of static.

Economy   Thrift; conservation.

Elastic   Two meanings: (a) the ability to regain original shape after being deformed; (b) the property of constant proportionality of stress to strain.

Element   A component or constituent part of a whole. Usually a distinct, separate entity.

Energy   Capacity for doing work. What is used up when work is done. Occurs in various forms: mechanical, heat, chemical, electrical, and so on.

Equilibrium   A balanced state or condition; usually used to describe a situation in which opposed effects neutralize each other to produce a net effect of zero.

Equivalent Static Force Analysis   The technique in which a dynamic effect is translated into a hypothetical (equivalent) static effect that produces a similar result.

Failure   The condition of becoming incapable of a particular function. May have partial as well as total connotations in structures. For example, a single connection may fail, but the structure might not collapse because of its ability to redistribute the load.

Fatigue   A structural failure that occurs as the result of a load applied and removed (or reversed) repeatedly over a long time or a large number of cycles.

Feasible Capable of being or likely to be accomplished.

Fit As a condition: well matched, adapted, suited, correct, or the right size. Not in conflict.

Flexible Two meanings: (a) limber, not stiff (as a fishing rod); (b) adaptable, or readily modified.

Footing A shallow bearing type foundation element, consisting of a pad or strip formed by pouring concrete directly into an excavation.

Form Shape. In structures, two ideas of form are important. First, the overall form of a structure, such as the profile of an arch. Second, the form of the parts, such as the cross section of the arch rib—square, hollow, I-shaped, and so forth.

Force An effort—as a push, pull, or twist—that tends to change the shape or the state of motion of something. Gravity, wind, water pressure, and thermal expansion are examples of sources of force. A force has the mathematical character of a vector. That is, it has magnitude (10 lb), direction (northwest) and sense (*from* southeast *to* northwest). In addition, it has location in space (4 ft from the end of a beam), and a particular point of application (hung from the bottom or placed on the top of the beam). A distinction is made between external force, such as the wind blowing on the building, and internal force, such as the compression in a column.

Fracture A break, usually resulting in actual separation of the material. A characteristic result of tension failure.

Frequency *See* Vibration.

Function Duty; intended use; capability.

Impact Action of striking or hitting.

Impulse An impelling force action, characterized by rapid acceleration or deceleration.

Indeterminable Irrevocably indefinite. Not capable of specific determination. *See* Determinate.

Indeterminate Indefinite; uncertain. In structural analysis usage denotes a condition that is indeterminable in some terms but may be solved by other means—either exactly or approximately. Distinguished from indeterminable by this notion of solution or approximation by other means.

Inertia *See* Mass.

Integration The bringing into association of distinct but related elements or systems. Thus the plumbing, wiring, ventilating ducts, elevators, and stairs must be integrated with the structure in the building whole.

Intuition Direct perception, independent of any conscious reasoning process.

Joist *See* Beam.

Lateral To the side or from the side. Often used to refer to something that is perpendicular to a major axis or direction. In comparison to vertical gravity forces, effects of wind and earthquakes and horizontally directed soil pressures are called lateral effects.

Live load *See* Load.

Load Active force, or combination of forces, exerted on a structure. *Dead load* is permanent gravity load, including the weight of the structure. *Live load* is any load component that is not permanent, including those of wind, earthquakes, temperature effects, and moisture fluctuations, as well as gravity forces that are not permanent.

Macro- Implies upper limits of scale involvement; large, excessive. *See* Micro-.

Mass The dynamic property of an object that causes it to resist changes in its state of motion. This resistance is called *inertia*.

The magnitude of mass per unit of volume of the object is called its *density*. Dynamic force is defined as mass times acceleration, or $F = ma$. Weight is defined as force produced by the acceleration of gravity; thus $W = mg$.

Micro-   Implies lower limit of scale involvement. Precise meaning: "very small." *See* Macro-.

Member   One of the distinct parts of an assemblage. *See* Component and Element.

Moment   Action tending to produce turning or rotation. Product of a force and a lever arm, gives a unit of force times distance (for example, pound-feet). Bending moment causes curvature; torsional moment causes twisting.

Motion   The process of changing position or location. Motion along a line is called translation; motion of turning is called rotation. Time rate of motion is called speed or velocity. Time rate of change of velocity is called acceleration.

Optimal   Best; most satisfying. The best solution to a set of criteria is the optimal solution. When the criteria have opposed values, there may be no single optimal solution.

Particle   A minute part. In structures, usually an extremely small piece of material, slightly bigger than molecular size.

Period   *See* Vibration.

Pier   A compression support element of rather stout (versus slender) proportions. Also a deep foundation element that is placed in an excavation rather than being driven into position. Although it actually refers to a particular method of excavation, the term *caisson* is commonly used to describe a pier foundation.

Pile   A deep foundation element, consisting of a shaftlike object that is driven into the ground. *Friction piles* develop resistance to both downward and upward

(uplift) loads through the development of friction between the soil and the pile surface. *End-bearing piles* are driven so that their tips are seated in a low-lying layer of rock or very hard soil.

Plastic   In stress analysis refers to stress–strain behavior beyond the elastic range. Plastic deformation usually implies some permanent shape change.

Rational   Allowing the application of reason. Reasonable, sensible. A rational analysis is one that proceeds without recourse to intuition or unwarranted assumptions.

Reaction   Response. In structures, the response of the structure to loads; the response of the supports to the action of the structure. *The reactions* usually refers to the components of force developed at the supports.

Reinforce   To strengthen; usually by adding something.

Resilience   The measurement of the absorption of dynamic energy by a structure without permanent deformation or fracture. *See* Toughness.

Resonance   *See* Vibration.

Retaining Wall   A structure used to brace a vertical cut at a change in elevation of the ground surface. The term is commonly used to refer to a *cantilever retaining wall*, a freestanding structure consisting only of a wall and its footing, although basement walls also serve a retaining function.

Rigidity   Quality of resistance to movement. Structures that are not rigid are flexible.

Rotation   Motion of turning.

Safety   Relative unlikelihood of failure. The *safety factor* is the ratio of the total capacity of a structure to the actual demand on the structure.

Scale   A reference of dimensional comparison. A model may be a scaled reproduction of an object. Large scale, as a model of a molecule; or small scale, as a model of a building.

Section   The two-dimensional profile obtained by passing a plane through a form. *Cross section* implies a section at right angles to another section or to the linear axis of an element.

Seismic   Pertaining to, or caused by, ground shock such as that caused by an earthquake.

Settlement   The downward movement of a foundation caused by the loads and their effects on the supporting soil.

Shear   Force that causes adjacent particles of a material to slide in relation to each other.

Sign   Algebraic notation of sense. Three cases: positive, negative, neutral. Relates to direction of force—if up is positive, down is negative; or to stress: if tension is positive, compression in the same direction is negative.

Simulation   Act of pretending, feigning, or impersonating. In structural analysis it refers to the artificial representation of a structural behavior or loading condition.

Slenderness   Relative thinness. In structures, the quality of flexibility or lack of buckling resistance is inferred by extreme slenderness.

Stability   The quality of being stable, or having the capability of remaining in position. Lack of sufficient support is a cause of external instability. *Elastic stability* refers to the phenomenon of buckling of slender compression elements.

Static   State of being at rest, having no motion. *See* Dynamic.

Stiffness   The quality of resistance to deformation on the part of a material, a component member of a structure, or the whole structure. The magnitude of the stress–strain ratio is a measurement of the stiffness of a material. The relative actual deflection of a beam is a measure of its stiffness. May also refer to resistance to dynamic movements of bounce, vibration, and so forth.

Strain   Change in shape of a material because of stress, expressed as a ratio or percentage. Accumulates in total movement of the structure, such as elongation, shortening, curvature, or twisting. Stress and strain are interdependent and inseparable.

Strength   Capacity to resist force.

Strength Design Method   One of the two fundamental techniques for assuring a margin of safety for a structure. *Stress design*, also called *working stress design*, is performed by analyzing for stresses produced by the estimated actual usage loads and assigning limits for the stresses that are below the ultimate capacity of the materials by some margin. *Strength design*, also called *ultimate* strength design, is performed by multiplying the actual loads by the desired factor of safety and then proceeding to design a structure that will have that load as its ultimate failure load.

Stress   Product of internal force; actually measured in terms of force per unit area. Three basic types: tension, compression, and shear. *See* Strain.

Structure   That which gives form to something and works to resist changes in the form from the action of various forces.

Stud   One of a set of small closely spaced columns used to define a framed wall structure.

Synthesis   The process of combining a set of component elements into a whole. Opposite of analysis.

System   An ordered assemblage.

Tension   Force that tends to separate adjacent parts of a material and produce stretching.

Torsion   Twisting moment, such as that exerted on a screw by the screwdriver.

Toughness The measurement of the total dynamic energy capacity of a structure, up to the point of complete failure. *See* Resilience.

Translation Motion of a body along a line without rotation, or turning.

Truss An articulated framework of linear elements that attains stability through triangular formations of the elements.

Ultimate Load The absolute maximum magnitude of load that a structure can sustain, limited only by ultimate failure.

Vector A mathematical quantity having direction as well as magnitude and sign (+ or −). Comparison is made to scalar quantities having only magnitude and sign. Thus time, temperature, length, and cost are scalar quantities; force, velocity, and the position of one point relative to another are all vector quantities. A vector may be graphically represented by an arrow with its length proportional to the magnitude, the angle of its line indicating the direction, and the arrowhead representing the sign (also called sense). *See* Motion.

Velocity Time rate of motion; speed. *See* Motion.

Vibration The cyclic, rhythmic motion of an object such as a spring. Occurs when the object is displaced from some neutral position and seeks to restore itself to a state of equilibrium when released. In its purest form it occurs as a harmonic motion with a characteristic behavior described by the cosine form of the displacement–time graph of the motion. The magnitude of linear displacement from the neutral position is called the *amplitude*. The time elapsed for one full cycle of motion is called the *period*. The number of cycles occurring in one second is called the *frequency*. Effects that tend to reduce the amplitude of successive cycles are called *damping*. The progressive increase of amplitude in successive cycles is called a *resonant effect*.

Visualize To create a mental image; to make perceptible to the mind.

Working Load The load condition created by the actual usage of the structure.

Working Stress Design Method *See* Strength design method.

Exercises

The following material is provided for those who use this book as a text.

KEY WORDS AND TERMS

Chapter 1 Feasibility, integration, optimization, safety, strength design method, structure, working stress design method.

Chapter 2 Adjacency, bearing wall, curtain wall, lateral bracing, partition, shear wall, substructure, superstructure.

Chapter 3 Bending, buckling, compression, creep, damping, dead load, dynamic, equilibrium, inertia, internal force, live load, load, load dispersion, mass, modulus of elasticity, moment, period of vibration, reaction, resonance, shear, stability, static, stiffness, strain, strength, stress, tension, torsion.

Chapter 5 Arch, geodesic dome, lamella structure, monopode structure, post and beam, rigid frame, surface structure, truss.

Chapter 6 Caisson, pier, pile, rock, shallow bearing foundation, soil.

QUESTIONS

Chapter 1

1 What are the main concerns for the building structure during a fire?
2 What is the purpose of the safety factor in structural design?
3 Why is the cost of the structure itself not necessarily a major determining factor in structural design?
4 What are some of the reasons that the optimization of structures in terms of efficiency of behavior under load is not always possible?

Chapter 2

1 What is meant by the description of the building skin as a selective filter?
2 What is usually meant when a wall is described as nonstructural?
3 Why is the term "flat roof" usually not accurate?
4 What are some of the structural problems that occur when a building has more than one story?
5 Why is the depth of the floor structure in multistoried buildings usually strongly limited?
6 What are the structural constraints that derive from adjacency situations in buildings?

Chapter 3

1 How can a structure fail to perform its architectural purposes even though it may resist the loads with an adequate factor of safety?
2 Describe the various effects of wind on buildings.
3ˑ What constitutes the external force system that operates on a structure?

4 Why is the strength of the material not a significant factor in the buckling of slender structures under compression?

5 Why do we say that all forms of stress (tension, compression and shear) exist whenever any internal force action occurs?

6 What are some sources of damping of the vibration of building structures?

Chapter 5

1 What is the difference between a rigid frame and an ordinary post and beam system?

2 What is the difference between the methods of pretensioning and posttensioning for prestressing concrete?

3 What is the significance of the rise-to-span ratio for an arch?

ASSIGNMENTS

1 For each of the basic structural materials (wood, steel, concrete and masonry) list both limitations and advantages in their uses for building structures.

2 For each of the limitations listed in (1), describe what measures (if any) can be taken to overcome them.

3 Find a building that is just beginning to be constructed. Visit the site periodically and photograph the progress of the construction. Photograph the building from the same point on successive visits. Organize the photos or slides obtained into a report on the growth of the building structure.

4 Find a local building that has been built recently. Contact as many people who were involved in the design and construction as possible. Interview them and write a case study report on the design of the structure for the building.

5 The Make and Break: this is a classic assignment involving the actual construction of a structure to perform a specific assigned task. The following is an example; endless variations are possible: Design and build a structure to span 4 ft on a simple, horizontal span and to carry a concentrated load at the center of the span. End support is limited to vertical reactions only. Materials for the structure are limited to wood and paper, although any material may be used for connection of parts. The efficiency of the structure on a strength–weight basis is critical. Your structure will be weighed, load tested to destruction, and your score determined using the graph shown in the illustration.

DEMONSTRATION PROJECTS (for assignment or for classroom demonstration)

1 **Involvement** Buckling of a linear element as related to slenderness.
   Procedure Select a slender linear element (strip of wood, plastic, metal) and find its total compression resistance for various increments of length. Start with a ratio of length to thickness of at least 200 for the longest specimen.
   Find Relation of load capacity to length (or to length/thickness ratio.)

2 **Involvement** Bending resistance related to shape.
   Procedure Test the bending resistance of a linear element on a single span when subjected to a load at the center of the span. Test elements of the same material and same total cross-sectional area, but with different shapes and different orientations to the load. Both bending strength (load capacity) and stiffness (deflection) may be tested.
   Find Correlation of bending resistance and shape in beams.

3 **Involvement** Bending and span.
   Procedure Test a linear element for

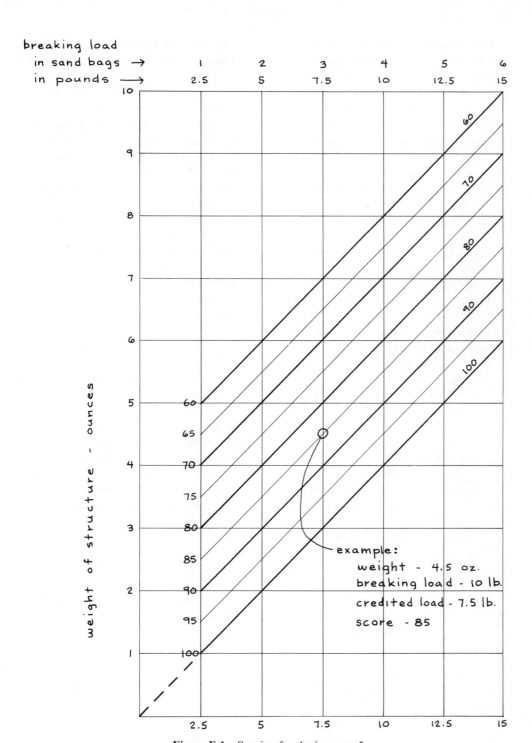

Figure E.1 Scoring for Assignment 5.

bending as in project No. 2. Test various specimens of the same material and cross section, but of increasing span length.

Find Relation of load capacity (and/or) deflection) to span length.

4 **Involvement** Bending resistance and support restraint.

Procedure Test the bending resistance of a linear element as in project No. 2. Test the same element on the. same span, but with three different conditions at the supports, as follows: (a) both ends free to turn, (b) one end clamped to prevent turning, (c) both ends clamped.

Find Effect of end restraint on load capacity (and/or deflection).

5 **Involvement** One-way versus two-way spanning. Effect of ratio of span lengths in rectangular two-way spans.

Procedure Test a thin planar element in bending (a sheet of cardboard, glass, plastic, metal) with a single load at the center of the span. Test specimens with the following shapes and support conditions at the edges: (a) square sheet, two opposite edges supported; (b) square sheet, three edges supported; (c) square sheet, four edges supported; (d) rectangular sheet with the small dimension the same as in (c) and the long dimension a multiple of the short of increasing magnitude in successive specimens: 1.25, 1.5, 1.75, 2.0, 2.5, and so on.

Find Comparison of effectiveness of one-way and two-way spanning. Relation of panel dimension ratio to effectiveness of two-way action in rectangular panels.

6 **Involvement** Torsion resistance of various cross-sectional shapes.

Procedure Test various linear elements of the same material and the same total cross-sectional area, but with different shapes. Fix one end and twist the other end without causing bending. Measure the twisting force for total load capacity or for some constant increment of rotation.

Find Effectiveness of various cross-sectional shapes in torsion.

7 **Involvement** Sag ratio of cables.

Procedure Test a tension element (string, wire, chain) for its total load resistance with various ratios of sag to span. Test by supporting the two ends and loading at the center.

Find Relation of sag ratio (sag to span) and load capacity.

8 **Involvement** Rise-to-span ratio in arches.

Procedure Test a flexible sheet (cardboard, plastic, aluminum) for its resistance to load in arch action. Attach two blocks to a base and bend the sheet to form an arch, kicking against the blocks. Load with a weight at the center of the arch, carefully avoiding any concentrated load effect at the point of load. Test specimens with various span-to-rise ratios.

Find Mode of failure and effectiveness of arch for various ratios of rise to span.

Sources for Further Study

There is literally a mountain—an ever-growing mountain—of published material about structures. For those who wish to pursue this subject further, the following brief list of references is given. These sources may lead the motivated reader to the rest of the mountain of information. The comments made are strictly my personal assessments. Following the list is a key to the subject grouping of the books, which should be helpful to the reader in selecting those titles most useful for certain specific needs.

PERIODICALS

1 *Architectural Record.* Regularly has articles on technical subjects, case studies of significant buildings, and an occasional feature issue on technology. The bulk of each issue is advertising, which is sometimes more interesting and informative than the editorial material.

2 *Progressive Architecture.* The other major U.S. monthly architecture magazine. Also has technical articles, case studies, and features on technology, as well as numerous advertisement.

3 *Engineering News-Record.* The major weekly national news magazine of the construction business. Ads use less color; most articles are not stimulating to building designers. However, this is where you read about the structures that *didn't* work and

about all the awful problems encountered in creating the beautiful buildings shown in living color in the architectural magazines.

BOOKS

1 *American Building 2: The Environmental Forces That Shape It*, 2nd ed., rev., by James Marston Fitch (Houghton Mifflin, Boston, 1972). An influential work on aspects of human–environment interaction and the consequences of urban and architectural design. A plea for a more intelligent design of the built environment in terms of its effects on people.

2 *Architectural Graphic Standards*, by Charles G. Ramsey and Harold R. Sleeper (Wiley, New York, 1981, 7th ed.). A classic reference for the building designer and draftsman on construction details.

3 *Architectural Structures: An Introduction to Structural Mechanics*, by Henry J. Cowan (American Elsevier, New York 1971). A comprehensive text on structures, including both basic mathematical analysis and general considerations of architectural functions of structures.

4 *Building Construction Handbook*, by Frederick S. Merritt (McGraw-Hill, New York, 1975, 3rd ed.). An encyclopedic handbook on many aspects of building technology. Discusses basic principles, design examples, illustrations, data, bibliographies.

5 *Building Construction Illustrated*, by Frank Ching (Van Nostrand-Reinhold,

Princeton, N.J., 1975). Illustrates the form and detail of ordinary building systems for small to medium scale structures.

6   *Building Structures: Elementary Analysis and Design*, by R. E. Shaeffer (Prentice-Hall, Englewood Cliffs, N.J., 1980). A general, comprehensive treatment of applied mechanics and the procedures and issues of the design of building structures. Uses SI units throughout. An excellent basic text for persons lacking a thorough engineering background.

7   *Construction Materials and Processes*, by Don Watson (McGraw-Hill, New York, 1978, 2nd ed.). A comprehensive treatment of the materials, products and processes used for building construction, with some insight into the basic processes of material production.

8   *The Dymaxion World of Buckminster Fuller*, by Robert Marks (Van Nostrand-Reinhold, Princeton, N.J., 1960). A study of the life and work of one of the most stimulating (though somewhat enigmatic) men in the area of design. Documents Fuller's development of the now famous tensegrity and geodesic systems.

9   *Emerging Form in Architecture: Conversations with Lev Zetlin*, by Forrest Wilson (Cahners, Boston, Mass., 1975). Result of an ongoing ten year conversation between an architect–writer and a highly creative engineering designer. Contains discussions and illustrations of many highly innovative structures.

10 *Great Architecture of the World*, edited by John Julius Norwich (Random House, New York, 1975). A treatment of architecture around the world and down through the ages. Noteworthy for its many isometric cutaway drawings that explain the construction of buildings, both ancient and modern.

11 *Kinetic Architecture*, by William Zuk and Roger H. Clark (Van Nostrand-Reinhold, Princeton, N.J., 1970). An illustrated study of the response of physical structures to requirements for change. Discusses adaptable, movable, expandable, retractable, demountable, flexible, and disposable systems.

12 *Robert Maillart*, by Max Bill (D'Architec-

ture—Artemis, Zurich, 1949). A study of the life and work of a highly creative and ingenious engineer who designed and built many innovative structures in the early part of this century.

13 *On Growth and Form*, by D'Arcy Wentworth Thomson, abridged edition by John Tyler Bonner (Cambridge University Press, New York, 1961). A stimulating study of the relations between form and function in biological structures. Analogies are made to human systems of cellular, shell, and skeletal form.

14 *Frei Otto: Form and Structure*, by Philip Drew (Westview Press, Boulder, Colo., 1976). A profusely illustrated discussion of the work of one of the most famous researchers and innovative designers in the development of tents, tension membranes, cable nets, and other tension structures.

15 *Philosophy of Structures*, by Eduardo Torroja (University of California Press, Berkeley, 1958). The credo, teachings, and design concepts of one of the greatest structural engineers of our times.

16 *Pier Luigi Nervi: Buildings, Projects, Structures, 1953-1963*, by Pier Luigi Nervi (Praeger, New York, 1963). A dramatically illustrated study of the work of a great contemporary designer-builder.

17 *Pneumatic Structures: A Handbook of Inflatable Architecture*, by Thomas Herzog (Oxford University Press, New York, 1976). Profusely illustrated treatment of the work of designers all over the world. Categorizes types of systems and explains basic concepts and problems.

18 *Simplified Building Design for Wind and Earthquake Forces*, by James Ambrose and Dimitry Vergun (Wiley, New York, 1980). Discusses the basic effects of wind and earthquakes on buildings, the use of current codes and design standards, and the design procedures for ordinary systems of bracing. Written for persons with a limited background in engineering analysis and design.

19 *Simplified Design of Building Structures*, by James Ambrose (Wiley, New York, 1979). Discusses and illustrates the design of the structure for three example buildings; proceding from architectural sketches

through structural calculations to an illustration of the construction details for the finished structure.

20 *Simplified Engineering for Architects and Builders*, by Harry Parker (Wiley, New York, 1975, 5th ed.). A useful digest of elementary structural engineering, from statics to the design of basic elements of wood, steel, and concrete. Handy because of its compactness, comprehensiveness, and use of simple mathematics. Widely used for years (together with other volumes in the Parker "simplified" series) by architects and other nonengineers with practical interest in simple structural engineering.

21 *Structure and Architectural Design*, by Philip A. Corkill, Homer L. Puderbaugh, and H. Keith Sawyers of the University of Nebraska (Sernoll, Inc., Iowa City, Iowa, 1974, 5th ed.). A profusely illustrated, nonmathematical treatment of basic structural principles and systems. Intended to provide a visually oriented foundation of knowledge and appreciation for the beginning student in building design.

22 *Structure and Form in Modern Architecture*, by Curt Siegel (Van Nostrand-Reinhold, Princeton, N.J., 1962). A study of various concepts of form in contemporary structures and of relations between structural form and function, construction techniques, and architectural planning and detailing.

23 *Structure in Architecture*, by Mario Salvadori and Robert Heller (Prentice-Hall, Englewood Cliffs, N.J., 1975, 2nd ed.). An excellent, nonmathematical presentation of principles of structures. Especially useful for visualization of structural behavior of rigid frames, two-way spanning slabs and grids, thin shells, and folded plates.

24 *Structure in Art and in Science*, edited by Gyorgy Kepes (George Braziller, New York, 1965). A collection of provocative and stimulating essays on the meaning of structure by a number of outstanding artists, scientists, and design professionals.

25 *Structure in Nature Is a Strategy for Design*, by Peter Pearce (MIT Press, Cambridge, Mass., 1978). A profound study of form, structure, pattern, growth, and assemblage in nature and its implications and

potentialities for manmade structures. Follows the tradition of previous work by D'Arcy Thomson, Konrad Wachsmann, Charles Eames, and Buckminster Fuller.

26 *Structure Systems*, by Heinrich Engel (Praeger, New York, 1968). An excellent illustrated discussion of the nature of various structural systems with studies of the generation of complex systems.

27 *Structure: The Essence of Architecture*, by Forrest Wilson (Van Nostrand-Reinhold, Princeton, N.J., 1971). A mildly tongue-in-cheek treatment of basic concepts of structures and their influence on the development of architectural form, traditions, styles, and techniques of construction and design.

28 *Structures*, by Pier Luigi Nervi (McGraw-Hill, New York, 1956). A short presentation of Nervi's philosophy on subjects including client relations, education of designers, theory of structures, and building with concrete. Illustrations show significant work by Nervi before 1957. *See also* Reference 16.

29 *Structures: An Architect's Approach*, by H. Seymour Howard, Jr. (McGraw-Hill, New York, 1966). An analytical study of seven buildings in terms of their structural solutions.

30 *The Structures of Eduardo Torroja*, by Eduardo Torroja (McGraw-Hill, New York, 1958). Case studies of his own work by a great structural engineer. *See also* Reference 15.

31 *Time-Saver Standards for Architectural Design Data*, by John H. Callender (McGraw-Hill, New York, 1974, 5th ed.). An encyclopedia on building design. Text discussion, illustrations, and data on various aspects of building planning, construction materials and details, structures, building equipment, site planning, and so on. Extensive bibliography in each section.

32 *The Turning Point of Building: Structure and Design*, by Konrad Wachsmann (Van Nostrand-Reinhold, Princeton, N.J., 1961) The work and teachings of a designer-teacher-philosopher, famous for his work in industrialized building processes, modular systems of assemblage, and space structures.

Subject–Use Key for Books Listed.

	relationships of structures to architecture	nonmathematical treatment of structural concepts	mathematical analysis of structures	engineering design of building structures	general technical information about building structures	illustration, and/or discussion of actual cases of building structures: design and construction	design techniques, teachings, and personal philosophies of individuals
1	•	•					•
2					•		
3			•	•			
4				•	•		
5					•		
6	•		•	•			
7					•		
8						•	•
9						•	•
10	•						
11						•	
12						•	•
13		•					•
14						•	•
15							•
16						•	•
17						•	
18			•	•			
19			•	•			
20			•	•			
21	•	•					
22	•						
23	•	•					
24							•
25	•	•				•	•
26	•	•				•	
27	•	•					•
28						•	•
29	•		•	•		•	
30						•	•
31					•		
32			•			•	•

134

Index